EXCELLENT UNIVERSITY TEACHING

Excellent University Teaching

David Kember, Rosa Ma, Carmel McNaught
and
18 excellent teachers

☆ *David Ahlstrom* ☆ *Andrew Chan* ☆ *Francis Chan*
☆ *Chan Hung Kan* ☆ *Gregory Cheng* ☆ *Gordon Cheung*
☆ *Chu Ming Chung* ☆ *Fan Jianqing* ☆ *Patrick Lau*
☆ *John Chi Kin Lee* ☆ *Kenneth Leung* ☆ *Leung Sing Fai*
☆ *Soung Liew* ☆ *Lo Wai Luen* ☆ *John Lui*
☆ *Gordon Mathews* ☆ *Allan Walker* ☆ *Zhang Shuzhong*

The Chinese University Press

Excellent University Teaching
By David Kember, Rosa Ma, Carmel McNaught
and 18 excellent teachers

© David Kember, Rosa Ma, Carmel McNaught,
David Ahlstrom, Andrew Chan, Francis Chan,
Chan Hung Kan, Gregory Cheng, Gordon Cheung,
Chu Ming Chung, Fan Jianqing, Patrick Lau,
John Chi Kin Lee, Kenneth Leung, Leung Sing Fai,
Soung Liew, Lo Wai Luen, John Lui, Gordon Mathews,
Allan Walker and Zhang Shuzhong, 2006

ISBN 962–996–267–5

THE CHINESE UNIVERSITY PRESS
The Chinese University of Hong Kong
SHA TIN, N.T., HONG KONG
Fax: +852 2603 6692
+852 2603 7355
E-mail: cup@cuhk.edu.hk
Web-site: www.chineseupress.com

Printed in Hong Kong

Table of Contents

Foreword

It is a delight to see this volume on Excellent University Teaching coming off the press. First of all, this volume is a celebration of excellent teaching, giving the exemplary teachers the recognition that they so richly deserve. But there is a much more important aim—through disseminating this systematic and objective analysis of the traits, attitudes and practices that lead to excellence, it is the hope that the practices of these exemplary teachers will come to be widely adopted as targets and models, and that in time excellence in teaching will not be a rare gem, but the norm in universities.

Reading through these accounts, one cannot avoid noticing the one pervasive trait common to all the excellent teachers portrayed in this volume—they are all reflective about their own teaching, and they are always seeking to learn and improve. Indeed, participation in the present project has probably helped them to clarify their own thoughts on teaching. The picture that they collectively paint should assist many other teachers to reflect on their own practice and become much more effective in their own roles as teachers.

It is very much the hope that the same would be true of teaching units as well—that they become more effective in their roles through self-reflection. And that is the reason why the University has adopted a systematic framework in which departments are urged to engage in self-examination based on evidence. This book will be a valuable instrument in helping all units understand and therefore benefit from the process.

David, Rosa and Carmel have our gratitude for taking up this task, and for bringing together the voices of our excellent teachers into a coherent chorus. I urge all to listen, and I look forward to significant improvements, both individual and system-wide, that would be found in a future study.

Kenneth Young
Pro-Vice-Chancellor &
Chairman, Senate Committee on Teaching and Learning
The Chinese University of Hong Kong

Acknowledgements

and Explanation of How the Book was Written

In a book with so many authors and contributors, it was not immediately obvious who would acknowledge who. I (David), as the first named author, have taken the initiative of writing the acknowledgement myself and using it as an opportunity to explain how the unusually large team has worked together to produce the book. At the same time due acknowledgement is paid to other contributions.

Carmel initiated the project by obtaining a generous grant from the directly assigned portion of the University Grant Committee of Hong Kong's Teaching Development Grants. The funding was used to employ Rosa to conduct interviews with 18 teachers who had been awarded the Vice-Chancellor's Award for Exemplary Teaching.

Initially the project was aiming to produce a set of stories, one for each of the 18 teachers. The first stories were fascinating, but after a few they became rather similar. I then came on the scene and started to analyse the set of interviews for common themes. This worked well; so the book started to take on the current shape.

Wading through a very thick pile of paper to analyse qualitative data can be a tedious task. For this project it was enjoyable because of the lively and interesting accounts of their teaching beliefs and practices told by the 18 teachers, with the help of Rosa's skilled prompting. The many and lengthy quotations all identify the teacher whose interview they came from, and this means that all the teachers become associate authors.

Carmel was responsible for copy editing and some of the introductory writing. We are all very grateful to Teresa Lo for textual design and graphics. We would also like to thank The Chinese University Press for publishing the book.

David Kember

Overview

There are several purposes to this book. Primarily, it was written to celebrate the work of exemplary teachers at The Chinese University of Hong Kong (CUHK). It is based on detailed interviews with 18 of the teachers who have been awarded the Vice-Chancellor's Exemplary Teaching Award at CUHK. The voice of these teachers is clear and vibrant in the book, through extensive quotations from the interview transcripts.

Another purpose was to listen to the collective voices of these teachers and make explicit the principles that informed the teaching of these excellent teachers. The synergy between these teachers from all faculties of the University is very clear. They may differ in the choice of specific strategies to use in their classrooms but the same set of principles underlies all of their actions.

A third follow-on purpose is to present these principles of teaching in a way which will make them accessible and useful to a wide range of university teachers—at CUHK, elsewhere in Hong Kong and China, and also in other nations of the world.

The book has three sections. The introductory section introduces the readers to current ideas about excellence in teaching. There is also a detailed description of the methodology of this study. Establishing the credibility of a study of this nature is essential to it being accepted. The bulk of the book (Chapters 3 to 7) is a progressive elucidation of the principles of excellent teaching. These principles cover all aspects of teaching.

Planning at both the curriculum and lesson level is tackled first. In planning for teaching the excellent teachers make use of a four-element curriculum development model—learning outcomes, content, learning activities and feedback for evaluation. The coherence between all aspects of their teaching is a strong feature of their teaching.

While many university teachers select the content for their courses only in terms of the coverage of the discipline area, our exemplary teachers have more holistic principles. In Chapter 4 these principles are explored. Excellent teachers select content which aids the learning of fundamental concepts; can help establish the relevance of the material in each course; and assists students in becoming independent, critical lifelong learners.

There are many books written about teaching methods. The added contribution of Chapter 5 is that it goes beyond providing teaching tips to an exposition of a rationale for deciding on appropriate teaching strategies. Excellent teachers base their choice of teaching strategies on an overall principle of engaging students in the learning process. They therefore put time into knowing their students as individuals. Their teaching is interactive and students have active roles to play in their classes. In Chapter 6, a range of excellent teaching strategies is explored.

The students of our exemplary teachers are enthusiastic and motivated to learn. In Chapter 7 the strategies used to motivate students are outlined and discussed in some detail. The final chapter of this middle section focuses on how these excellent teachers grew and developed their perceptions of their role and their repertoire of strategies. The advice they give is wide-ranging and shows how open, enquiring and self-reflective these teachers are. They are also disciplined as they seek and maintain excellence in research as well in a synergistic fashion.

The final two chapters move away from the detailed work of a teacher to see if our exemplary teachers can also assist understanding of some other aspects of higher education. Chapter 8 addresses the question of whether quality in teaching is culturally specific, whether there are differences between concepts of teaching excellence in Chinese and Western universities. In a globalized world this question is gaining increasing attention. The excellent university teachers in this study are part of a global university culture, and hence it follows that the derived principles of good teaching should be widely applicable. The principles of excellent teaching are therefore presented as a model of good practice in university teaching for any reputable university.

In the final chapter, implications of the principles of excellent teaching for learning enhancement are investigated. How can we apply these principles in the design and delivery of professional development schemes for university teachers? What are the lessons for the formulation and implementation of university teaching and learning quality assurance schemes? We end by coming full circle to reflect on ways in which CUHK might enhance its own Exemplary Teaching Award scheme.

The book is offered to colleagues teaching in universities anywhere. It is our hope that the wisdom and practice of these CUHK teachers will be of value and use to all university teachers.

Principles of Excellent Teaching

Planning Teaching and Courses

1. Planning for teaching includes articulating expected learning outcomes, selecting learning activities and seeking feedback for evaluation from students, as well as determining content.

2. When planning courses it is necessary to anticipate the needs of the students.

3. Teachers should make a detailed plan of each lesson, including learning activities, but then be prepared to flexibly adapt the plan in the light of students' responses.

What is Taught

4. Teachers should concentrate on teaching key concepts, rather than detail, and make the fundamental points explicit.

5. Teachers should select content which students can perceive as relevant and show how it is relevant.

6. What is taught should take into account students' need to develop the ability to learn for themselves. Self-managed learning ability can be nurtured through student-centred approaches to teaching.

7. Exposing students to conflicting theories helps develop more sophisticated beliefs about knowledge, and this facilitates the development of important graduate capabilities.

How it is Taught

8. Good teachers develop a relationship with their students by getting to know them as individuals.

9. A vital constituent of excellent teaching is interaction in class between the teachers and their students, and the promotion of discussion among students.

10. Excellent teachers use a variety of teaching methods appropriate to the desired learning outcomes.

11. Exemplary teachers use a variety of methods of assessment which are valid tests of the planned learning outcomes. These assessment strategies are also consistent with encouraging the development of these outcomes.

Motivating Students

12.   Excellent teachers accept that they have a responsibility to motivate their students.

13.   Good teachers have high expectations of students.

14.   Strategies for motivating students include:
- the teacher displaying enthusiasm;
- employing a variety of active learning approaches;
- making classes enjoyable;
- using relevant and interesting material; and
- praising students when high expectations are met.

Development as a Teacher

15.   Good teaching can be developed through
- learning from past teachers;
- exchanging ideas with colleagues; and
- attending workshops.

16.   To improve teaching it is necessary to gather feedback, reflect upon it and then act on the reflections.

17.   The tension between teaching and research can be handled by recognizing the importance of teaching, and seeking synergies between teaching and research.

Chapter 1

What is Quality in Teaching?

There have been many attempts to define quality in higher education. In this chapter we provide a brief overview of this complex terrain. However, the main focus is on descriptions of quality in teaching, which is one facet of the overall judgment of the quality of a university. This chapter provides some background for this book where quality in teaching is investigated by exploring the characteristics of good teaching that are considered important by award-winning teachers at CUHK. These characteristics are framed as a set of principles of excellent teaching. The process whereby these principles are derived from the interviews is unfolded in Chapters 2 to 8. In Chapter 9 we will revisit some of the issues outlined in this chapter by considering the implications of this set of principles for university teaching, quality assurance and the professional development of university teachers.

Quality in a Changing University World

Universities are currently in an environment of intense change. They are being required to educate more students, from an increasing variety of backgrounds, with decreasing government funding. Universities are required to compete vigorously for student enrolments and external sources of funding. In this increasingly stressed environment the "quality agenda" has growing importance. Harvey and Green (1993) explored the idea that the definition of quality adopted by an individual or an organization depends on individual or collective beliefs about the meaning of quality. Broadly, these beliefs range from an instrumental focus on accountability for public funds to a belief that a focus on matters of quality can be a transformative influence within higher education. This is a very broad range and points to one major challenge in discussing quality issues: namely the language used to describe quality. On the American Society for Quality website, quality is described as "a subjective term for which each person has his or her own definition." There is indeed only one thing that all authors in the educational quality literature agree on, and that is that educational quality is a complex, multifaceted construct.

Writing in the United Kingdom, Green (1994) noted that quality can be viewed and measured from several perspectives. She used an analogy to a flow model of inputs, process and outputs. Measuring the output quality of graduates (either in economic terms of whether they get jobs, or in educational terms of their attainment of capabilities) is not sufficient. Understanding the characteristics of the students entering universities (inputs), and tracking the fitness and quality of the teaching and learning environments they operate within (process), is also essential. This awareness of the need to examine the totality of students' university experience in order to gauge educational quality is important.

While seeing quality as a multifaceted construct is useful, this "factory" model of inputs, process and outputs tends to be "value-free." In a value-free approach, there is an assumption that if enough factors are included in the model, then it will be possible to reach consensus about how best to define quality. However, quality is a value-laden construct and the idea of easily reaching consensus on a definition of quality is utopian. There are values associated with commonly used quality indicators and these need to be clarified. For example, an emphasis on minimum time for completion as a quality indicator can put pressure on teachers to lower their assessment standards; on the other hand, equity needs from a social justice perspective can exert pressure towards maximizing the number of places available.

Harvey and Knight (1996), also writing from within U.K. higher education, outlined a more specific focus on quality measurements as transformational power. They distinguished clearly between various quality indicators in their argument that it is wasteful and counterproductive to focus on quantitative indicators, such as costs and student numbers, without focusing on the effectiveness of student learning outcomes. They examined several definitions of quality, ranging from a traditional view that quality is related to exceptional or excellent standards to a more radical position of empowerment where quality is seen as transformational.

> Students are not products, customers, consumers, service users or clients—they are participants. Education is not a service for a customer ... but an ongoing process of transformation of the participant. (Harvey & Knight, 1996, p. 7)

As we will see, our exemplary teachers have this deeply student-centred transformative view of education.

On the other side of the Atlantic similar views are echoed in different words. Freed, Klugman, and Fife (2000) discussed quality as being an element of the culture of universities and described how a culture for academic excellence can be engendered by a holistic implementation of a set of quality principles. They emphasized the need for universities to move away from piecemeal planning towards a coherent plan. Their principles are focused more on organizational learning than on class teaching and learning but the synergies are clear. Educational quality and organizational quality are interdependent and both rely on the adoption of a set of appropriate principles. Bearing in mind this idea of interdependent principles, let us now turn to how various writers have defined principles for excellent teaching.

Views About Teaching and About Excellent Teaching

How are characteristics of excellent teaching and teachers described in the student learning literature? There are several lists of such characteristics. For the purposes of this chapter two criteria were used in selecting sets of characteristics to examine. The first consideration took into account the fact that the education literature of North America is often different in style and emphasis from that developed in the rest of the English-speaking world, for example the United Kingdom and Australia. In addition, there is relatively little cross-utilization of the two literatures through citation. It was therefore considered important to look at the characteristics of good teachers and teaching defined within both sets of literature. The other criterion was whether the authors of these descriptions are relatively well known within their own communities and perhaps more broadly. To that end, descriptions of good teachers and teaching that are outcomes of studies commissioned by government agencies or large professional organizations were sought. The final selection consisted of:

- A study commissioned in the United Kingdom by the Committee of Vice-Chancellors and Principals of U.K. universities (Elton & Partington, 1993). Lewis Elton is also a very well-known educational researcher;

- A U.K. government-funded study on recognizing and rewarding excellent teaching in U.K. universities (Gibbs & Habeshaw, 2002). Again, the authors have written widely in the teaching and learning literature; they are especially well known for the "53 series" which contains 13 books of useful tips for university teachers to use (e.g., Gibbs, Habeshaw, & Habeshaw, 1992);

- An Australian government-funded study on recognizing and rewarding good teaching in Australian universities (Ramsden, Margetson, Martin, & Clarke, 1995). However, the work of the first author is clearly based on earlier work in the United Kingdom (e.g., Entwistle & Ramsden, 1983);

- A very widely used book in Australia (and to some extent the United Kingdom) by Ramsden (1992);

- A review article by Feldman (1976). Feldman has a long career of work in teaching and learning in U.S. universities (e.g., Feldman & Newcomb, 1969; Feldman & Paulsen, 1994). This review was cited in an extensive review of the literature on student evaluations of university teaching by Marsh (1987); Marsh is a well-known researcher in the evaluation field;

- An often cited American Association of Higher Education bulletin on seven principles for good practice in undergraduate education (Chickering & Gamson, 1987); and

- An essay by a U.S. teacher who was the recipient of the prestigious Carnegie Professor of the Year Award (Beidler, 1997).

The number of characteristics of good teachers and teaching listed in these studies varied from 6 (Ramsden, 1992) to 32 (Gibbs & Habeshaw, 2002). These seven sets of characteristics differed in length and form, and so a "rough and ready" method of qualitative description was adopted. In order to look for patterns within these seven sets of characteristics, the lists were scanned. It was quite apparent that some characteristics focused on teachers' level of performance and some on learning needs and outcomes of students. Each characteristic was classified into one of the categories listed in Table 1. These categories were arrived at by an iterative process. There is undoubtedly overlap between the categories and the decision for listing any given characteristic was a "best fit" decision. In the last two columns in Table 1 the number of times a characteristic of this type was listed in the seven studies, and the resultant percentage for this type of characteristic in this sample, are provided. It should be stressed that this is only an indicative set of classifications but it does clearly illustrate the range of characteristics of good teachers and teaching used by the authors in this sample.

These seven studies describe characteristics which focus on a teacher's performance and knowledge, the relationships and interaction between teachers and students, and aspects of students' experiences. About one quarter of the stated characteristics are focused on a teacher's performance in specific courses and one quarter on the quality of the interactions between teachers and students. Teachers' preparation for teaching, and a focus on student motivation and learning are other strong features. This classification exercise thus reinforces the notion that quality in teaching is a multifaceted construct.

There was also variability in emphasis between the sets of characteristics. This is to be expected because these sets of characteristics were not empirically derived; rather they come from experiences and reflection which are more or less widely based within each of the studies used in this exercise. There is certainly no clear and consistent view of what constitutes quality in teaching and learning across these seven studies. One of the motivations for this study was that empirically deriving a set of characteristics or principles of good teaching may provide a more consistent and enduring framework for the quality literature.

Table 1.1. Classifications of Characteristics of Good Teaching in Seven Studies (With Illustrative Examples)

Category	Description of category	Illustrative examples		No. of times characteristic in this category listed in the seven studies	%
Teacher knowledge	Emphasis on teachers' subject knowledge and scholarship.	• Teacher's knowledge of the subject. • Teacher's intellectual expansiveness and breadth of coverage.	Feldman (1976)	10	10
Teacher design	Emphasis on teachers' preparation for teaching in terms of designing the curriculum. This includes articulating learning outcomes and designing assessment.	• Good teachers recognize the importance of context, and adapt their teaching accordingly. • Clear goals and intellectual challenge.	Ramsden et al. (1995) Ramsden (1992)	16	17
Teacher performance in the course(s) being taught	Emphasis on what teachers do in the classroom and in the contexts of the courses they teach.	• Quality of actual teaching activity, particularly for active learning. • Management of teaching.	Elton & Partington (1993)	26	27
Teacher performance in a wider context	Emphasis on what teachers do for teaching and learning in their institutions or for the teaching profession.	• Champions learning and teaching in the university. • Supports and collaborates with colleagues.	Gibbs & Habeshaw (2002)	5	5
Teacher–student interactions	This includes the quality of the relationship in general, feedback given by teachers to students on their learning, and feedback given by students to teachers on the design and conduct of the courses being studied.	• Encourages contacts between students and faculty. • Gives prompt feedback.	Chickering & Gamson (1987)	23	24
Student learning	Focus on students' personal conceptual understanding and development of appropriate skills.	• Try to give students confidence. • Try to motivate students by working within their incentive system.	Beidler (1997)	16	17
Total number of characteristics listed in the seven studies				96	100

Of course, principles of excellent teaching are interdependent. In this book the 18 teachers had different ways of expressing each of the 17 principles listed on pp. xi–xii. However, each teacher expressed all of these principles in her/his teaching.

Bain (2004) conducted a 15-year study of the thinking and practices of highly successful university educators in the United States. In this detailed study he used interviews, observations, as well as curriculum statements and materials. This rich data set results in an elegant essay about the practices of 63 selected excellent teachers. His discussion of how these teachers operate is one of rich description and his observations are congruent with the principles derived in this book. He portrays good teaching as a process of continual improvement,

> … as serious and important intellectual and creative work, as an endeavour that benefits from careful observation and close analysis, from revision and refinement, and from dialogues with colleagues and the critiques of peers. (p. 173)

Another of the aims of this book is to exemplify, within the context of CUHK, how the derived principles are played out in practice by our exemplary teachers in this process of striving for continual growth and improvement.

Views on Awards for Excellent Teachers

In the early 1990s in Australia some descriptive studies of the strategies used by award-winning university teachers were published (e.g., Dunkin, 1991). However, as McNaught and Anwyl (1992) noted in their report of award schemes at all Australian universities, many of the award schemes were not based on a broad enough base of data, especially student input. However, award schemes have now been in operation in many countries for a significant period of time and these awards do represent a consensus of opinion that award-winning teachers do show strong elements of excellence in their teaching. What is perhaps not clear is a more detailed understanding of how these teachers go about the process of planning, implementing and evaluating their teaching. This was one of the strong motivating reasons for this project.

The 44 narratives in the Ballantyne, Bain, and Packer (1997) volume attempt to convey the ways in which university teachers from a wide range of disciplines understand and enact connections between educational beliefs, contexts and practices. Healey (2000), writing on the scholarship of teaching, argued that the key to developing a scholarly approach is to embed the process in the disciplines. Most academic staff give their primary allegiance to their discipline or profession rather than their institution and see their own discipline as having unique characteristics. Research indicates that attitudes to teaching, patterns of communication, learning goals and learning styles vary between disciplines (Biglan, 1973; Donald, 1997; Kolb, 1994; Moses, 1990). Thus, an important question is whether concepts and models of good teaching will also vary between, as well as within, disciplines. Also, are there variations between different year levels, teaching contexts (large classes, tutorial groups, practical sessions, online teaching) and orientation of the programme (professional versus general)? To what extent do common principles underlie these disciplinary and contextual differences? Finding at least a partial answer to these questions was another key reason for this project.

So, this project arose from a desire to understand what principles underpinned the work of the exemplary teachers at our University. We wanted to understand disciplinary nuance; we wanted to examine the influence of teaching context and year level. Finally, we wanted to portray the work of these excellent teachers in a way that celebrates and acknowledges their achievements, and also makes their ideas and strategies accessible to other teachers at CUHK and elsewhere in the world.

Chapter 2

Method

The material in this book is based on interviews with 18 teachers awarded the Vice-Chancellor's Exemplary Teaching Award at CUHK. The award was instituted in the 1999–2000 academic year as a component of the University's way of recognizing the importance of, and rewarding, good teaching.

Each year one teacher from each of the seven faculties is given the award. As is common with decision-making and quality assurance procedures at CUHK, the selection process has been devolved. Each faculty takes responsibility for selecting exemplary teachers from its ranks and forwarding nominations to the Vice-Chancellor. Some of the faculties have further devolved the selection process by making awards within departments and then selecting the faculty nominee from these. The processes for selecting nominees are left to the faculties and so there is a degree of variation between them.

Selecting Excellent Teachers

Variations in method and criteria were found among individual departments and faculties in their process of selecting and nominating teachers for the award.

> We only take teaching evaluation as a reference. One reason is that some teaching is done in a serial manner. If the first teacher fails to teach well she or he may affect the next teacher. Even if the second teacher is doing a much better job, students may still have problems understanding since the foundation is weak, and they might rate the second as low as the first. Secondly, some teachers may appease students to avoid low ratings. Thirdly, there are students who do not attend classes and we cannot measure nonresponse.

> I am aware of all these. When we nominate, we first look at teachers who gain high ratings, then we will see what their nonresponse is. We will also consider other factors that affect teachers' performance, namely, class size, major or nonmajor classes, the hour of teaching—a class at 8:30 is likely to be received differently from that of 9:30 by students, and so forth. We look at all these factors and make adjustment with some statistical techniques. The outcome will narrow the search down to three or four persons. Then we consider each individual and see who finally deserve to be nominated. (Fan Jianqing – Statistics)

As shown in the above quotation, departments do take the nomination very seriously. In the Faculty of Business Administration, an equally comprehensive search was described:

The teaching evaluations of the past three years are considered. We use a pseudoscientific method whereby different programmes are factorized into overall unit marks. We have a committee which consists of the Dean and the two Associate Deans. The committee will then look at each individual profile: whether their teaching is comprehensive, that is, they aren't just good in teaching one subject but not the others; whether there are problems which are hidden behind the figures. We also look at response rates from students. These are the indicators we use and the Dean will nominate the best two to the VC. (Gordon Cheung – Management)

Peer reviews and course evaluations are common indicators of these selection processes. In the Faculty of Social Science, at least, a wide variety of other indicators are used in the selection processes:

Initially, it is based on the student course evaluation. It includes all subjects, old and new, of both undergraduate and postgraduate courses. Second, we read the recommendation by the department chair—a kind of peer evaluation. Third, we will consider the portfolio written by the nominated teachers stating their views on why they are being nominated. Does the teacher keep improving his/her teaching method? Innovativeness plays an important part in assessing teaching performance in this award.

We understand that effective teaching takes many different forms. It is not comparing alongside a checklist. We have to examine case by case and the committee will discuss: Why this one is better than the other? In what ways is this teacher better? Sometimes, it is really difficult to make that comparison. Ultimately, we ask ourselves: Do students find the teaching meaningful? Do students really learn? Student course evaluation, peer evaluation, supervisor evaluation and self-evaluation make up a thorough picture. (Kenneth Leung – Journalism)

Discursive Interviewing as the Appropriate Research Method

The interviews were conducted after the third round of awards. At this point in time 20 teachers had received this award and 18 of them were interviewed. This is a typical sample size for qualitative research, which rarely goes beyond a handful of informants, because of the time-consuming nature of data gathering and analysis. Richness and depth of insight are achieved at the expense of extensive sampling.

Research into teachers' beliefs, attitudes and conceptions of teaching, as well as their teaching approaches, has employed a combination of methods such as questionnaires, interviews and observations (Bennett, 1976; Galton, Simon, & Croll, 1980; Galton, Hargreaves, Comber, Wall, & Pell, 1999). In exploratory terms, questionnaires and observations only allow indirect inference to be drawn from the researcher's superimposed knowledge of the actor's reality (Shipman, 1981), whereas interviews enable a more direct access to the actor's beliefs and perceptions from their own standpoint (Kvale, 1994). Bruner (1990) stated that to understand how one's experience and one's acts are shaped by one's beliefs, a researcher needs to explore the social dimension in which the actor's beliefs are formed (Geertz, 1973).

To explore what constitutes excellent teaching and how the award-winning teachers developed themselves to the recent high standard, a semistructured interview was employed for the investigation. This is a kind of focused discourse in which the main themes of the research inquiry guide the discussion and the information gathered. The use of open-ended questions gives great freedom for informants to raise any issues naturally which are central to their concerns and that may have been left out by the researcher in the planning stage (Cohen & Manion, 1994). It is semistructured so that the research can accommodate both the key issues set out beforehand and the important relevant issues raised by the informant.

A potential problem with discourse is leading questions which could mislead answers. Burr (1995) argued that so long as orienting questions, discourse procedures, techniques and responses are made explicit and are open to public scrutiny, deliberately leading questions can be a good technique for orientating respondents in important directions, yielding new discoveries and worthwhile knowledge.

Burman and Parker (1993) argued that a discursive interview is a more objective research tool in a sense that it reflects the real nature of the object investigated by "letting the object speak." The problem of reporting and recalling biases, cognitive inconsistencies or even deception in a discourse can be checked by sufficient discursive procedures and techniques. Kvale (1994) and Yin (1994) suggested that by making the procedures, techniques and data explicit, researchers and readers can examine these biases or deceptions. This adds strength to the qualitative research methodology as quantitative methods would just leave these problems unexplored.

The very strength of qualitative discourse is its exploratory nature. It substantiates an investigative concept of validation (Glaser & Strauss, 1967) whereby validation is incorporated into the research process with continual cross-references to the credibility and plausibility of findings (Potter & Wetherell, 1994). Such a communicative and interactive approach enables the social actors, the teachers in this case, to reflect upon and become aware of their implicit beliefs and knowledge which influence their teaching behaviours. It can bring out the affective and value-laden implications of the personal context in which idiosyncratic associations, beliefs and perceptions become explicit, enabling an indepth analysis and a systematic reconstruction of phenomena.

Bearing in mind the above points, a set of interview questions was drafted as follows:

- How would you describe your area of exemplary practice?
- Can you highlight the main features of your practice for me?
- What are the really important ideas in your field that you want your students to learn?
- Please tell me about the most important influences on your life, particularly those persons or critical incidents that have influenced your professional development.
- How has your approach to teaching developed?
- What do you want to achieve through your teaching?
- What is good teaching in your view?
- What is poor teaching?
- Have you tried methods that didn't work?
- What is learning?
- Tell me about your students.
- Do you share your teaching ideas and methods with colleagues?
- What have we left out of your story?

The questions were used mainly as prompts to ensure that the main topics were covered. All the interviews were conducted by Rosa. The interviews were very conversational in style, as can be deduced from the extensive quotations. The interviewees spoke eloquently and at length on the topic of teaching and needed little in the way of questions or prompts. Except for the first leading question which initiated the discussion on the topic, the rest of the questions were asked in a sequence and manner that followed the natural flow of the interview. The exemplary teachers were very willing to share their beliefs and the issues which were central to their concern, particularly the tension between teaching and research and how they went about solving it. Ample descriptions of actual incidents were provided by the teachers as illustrations of the key points.

Interviewing the excellent teachers was an enjoyable task. One could feel the enthusiasm and dedication they had in teaching expressed in many different styles and personalities. It would be quite wrong to treat them as one self-selected homogenous group with some special predisposition to good teaching. Each of them had different emphases in their approach, while sharing some commonalities in practice. All of them were very busy scholars with other equally pressing commitments in research and service to the community. A common scenario was the interview being interrupted by telephone calls, students requesting assistance or colleagues requiring collaboration.

The interviews with the 18 exemplary teachers were quite lengthy, lasting on average 82 minutes of actual interviewing time (excluding the interruptions). The total range of time was 54 to 101 minutes. The richness of the dialogues revealed that related issues were explored in breadth and in depth during the interviews.

Twelve of the interviews were conducted in Cantonese and six in English. All interviews were recorded digitally with optimal sound quality.

Transcription and Translation

Where translation from Cantonese was required, the style and manner of speech was kept as close to the original as possible. Interviews in English were transcribed, with the result that there was a complete set of interview transcripts in English. All the translated transcripts were checked by Rosa and, where necessary, detail was checked with the interviewee. As a reliability check, regarding the translation, transcription and interpretation of meaning, each of the chapters in this book was sent to the interviewees for verification and feedback.

Analysis of Data

The analysis was principally based upon grounded theory (Glaser & Strauss, 1967; Lincoln & Guber, 1985). The essence of grounded theory is that the researchers do not impose preconceived frameworks or theories on the data; rather, theory emerges from the data, and so is grounded in it. The aim, in this case, was to characterize views of good teaching in a manner consistent with the data.

The use of grounded theory began with an intense examination of the set of transcripts by David. The interviews were quite long (the printout of the complete set amounted to 254 pages), and so searching through them for common constructs and themes was an intensive time-consuming task, as is common with the analysis of qualitative data.

As the reading and rereading progressed, marginal notes were pencilled in. Eventually these became the initial set of codings for themes and subthemes. There was found to be a high degree of consistency between the teachers as to what constituted quality in teaching. There was, however, an interesting variety in how the principles were applied and the ways they were described in the interviews.

In doing this initial search for grounded themes, use was made of the constant comparative method (Strauss & Corbin, 1990) to ensure that emerging theory was consistent with the whole sense of an interview. Following the constant comparative method implies that the analyst makes continuing reference to the whole interview rather than looking at sorted extracts. The result is that the parts of the interview selected as indicative of emerging constructs have their meaning referenced against the sense of the whole interview. The constant comparative method is, therefore, a guard against taking isolated comments out of context and a strategy for ensuring that the true underlying meaning of parts of an interview is identified.

The next step in the analysis was for Rosa to translate the marginal pencil comments into NVivo coding. NVivo (2000) is a computer programme which provides tools to assist the analysis of qualitative data. The strength of NVivo in analysing qualitative data is that it enables the handling of a voluminous body of text in which similar concepts can be encoded and structured. The programme has facilities for indexing, text-searching, using Boolean operations on defined index nodes, and combining data from several initially independent documents (Richards & Richards, 1991). It is, therefore, very effective for a project which has multiple data sources and anticipates outcomes with a wide variety of dimensions, as NVivo facilitates searches and comparison of data.

The translation of the marginal notes from the first round of analysis resulted in 66 coding categories defined with the NVivo hierarchical code numbering system. The process of Rosa entering these codes into the text file resulted in a check on David's initial analysis of the main themes. Any inconsistencies in interpretation were resolved through discussion. Coding the transcripts with NVivo also led to the data being more comprehensively analysed than in the initial examination, which inevitably concentrated upon spotting key constructs rather than inclusiveness.

Once the coding was complete it was then possible to sort the data according to the hierarchical node structure. A printout was then produced which had the data ordered in the form implied by the original coding structure. This brought together comments which had initially appeared to be on related themes.

The data in this form were then reanalysed by David. The essence of the reanalysis was an attempt to transform the original coded themes and subthemes into a more coherent and logical structure. Nodes in the hierarchical coding structure were shifted to make relationships clearer. Closely related coding nodes were merged or turned into a category and subcategory relationship. This process was performed partly by physically sorting the piles of paper and partly by drawing diagrams showing the desired structure.

A simplified and neater version of the originally hand-drawn diagram is shown in Table 2.1. The first column shows the main groupings of constructs, which subsequently became the five analysis chapters. The main themes are in the second column and the subthemes in the third column.

The NVivo coding was then modified by Rosa to follow the lines of the reanalysis. This recoding again allowed for a check on consistency of interpretation. The result was 41 finely tuned classification codes. Some of these do not appear in Table 2.1 as they refer to material which was subsequently decided to be outside the subject area of the book.

The recoded data set was then printed out following the order of the coding nodes. David then selected a set of quotations to form the framework for the five analysis chapters. Quotations were selected on the basis of being typical of the underlying meaning of the theme, and of the clarity with which the theme was explained and illuminated. The quotations are both more extensive and longer than in most writing based on qualitative research. Essentially each of the interviewees has become an associate author of the book, rather than being an anonymous interviewee, which is the normal practice in reporting qualitative data.

The process of writing was itself a part of the analysis. The main function of the writing was to provide a clear explanation of the themes which had emerged from the data. In their most reduced form these emerge as a set of principles of excellent teaching. The writing draws upon the quotations to show how they were derived. Also, the writing aims to explain and amplify the quotations through the process of setting them in a logical flow of discourse.

Some reordering of the structure took place during the writing as relationships between themes became clearer with the more detailed examination necessitated by the writing process. Comparison of Table 2.1 with the headings and subheadings in the following five chapters shows, though, that the structure which emerged from the second round of analysis proved quite enduring.

Verification Procedures

A common attack on qualitative discourse relates to bias in the interpretation of findings. To guard against idiosyncratic interpretations, the study employed an unusually high number of verification procedures. The checking of chapters by the interviewees has already been mentioned. Verification between the original two stages of analysis and the NVivo coding has also been described.

As the transcripts had been coded with NVivo it was possible to perform semiquantitative checking of number of interviewees making a point consistent with the main themes ensconced in the principles. A simple frequency count is a subordinate measure employed to illuminate and verify qualitative findings (Tam, 1993).

As the analysis chapters were completed each was sent to all interviewees with a request for them to confirm that their views were consistent with what was reported in the analysis. Some minor errors were noted and some positive feedback was received. No fundamental disagreement was reported back. We can, therefore, make the unusual claim for qualitative research of having all interviewees holding views consistent with the fundamental principles derived in the analysis.

Table 2.1. The Analytical Structure After the Second Stage

planning		
	principles	
	programme/course level	
	lesson level	
what		
	relevance	
	fundamental concepts	
	conflicting theories	
	capabilities	
		discipline/career-related
		learning to learn
how		
	engaging students in discussion	
	relating to students	
		building relationships
		knowing students
		adaptability in class
		feedback for improvement
	teaching methods	
		WebCT
		computer games
		professional application
		overseas visits
		group projects
		cases/PBL
		variety of approaches
	assessment	
motivation		
	make it enjoyable	
	making demands on students	
	variety of active learning	
	relevant content	
	enthusiasm of teacher	
development		
	through colleagues	
	modelling on past good teachers	
	self-reflection	
	feedback	
	attending workshops	
	handling teaching/research	
		importance of teaching
		relationship between two

Chapter 3

Planning Teaching and Courses

This is the first of five chapters which present the outcomes of the analysis of the interviews with the excellent teachers. The five chapters indicate the main topics which these exemplary teachers considered important in describing the nature of their teaching.

The analysis showed that, in spite of the range of disciplines and the variety in individual approaches, it was possible to derive a set of general principles which characterize excellence in teaching. In the five analysis chapters extensive quotations are used to substantiate the process of deriving the principles and to amplify and illuminate them.

Four Elements of Planning

When asked to plan a course, many academics think only of content. They are experts in their discipline, and so they concentrate upon selecting appropriate topics for the course in question and ordering them in a logical sequence. A curriculum document or syllabus, therefore, often consists of a list of content or topics to be covered in a course arranged in the order in which they are to be delivered in the lectures.

Some universities require curriculum planning documents to state objectives. The typical content-centred teacher commonly sees this as an unnecessary chore. As a consequence, the point of the exercise is often subverted by placing "The student will understand…" before each of the topics in the list of content. As a result the curriculum document effectively has two lists of content to be covered.

The excellent teachers, however, recognized that planning a successful course or programme involves more than just listing content. There is also a need to consider the learning outcomes which are expected and how the course will be taught.

> In the process, you have to decide what academic purpose and what activities are desirable. We will design some basic elements for them together with some textbooks, exercises or case studies. Built-in learning activities are essential, such as inviting CEOs to give talks, visiting the PRC, helping them to establish their networks, arranging summer internships, offering free consultation to companies so students can gain solid work experience through their voluntary work, and so forth. I'll try to aggregate all the relevant elements, not only concentrating on text-based teaching.

We don't stop at the "here" and "now". We have to proactively think of the future trend of this subject five years down the line. Sometimes, things change so rapidly that we'll need to review and project to the future within three years, or even one year, as people's perceptions may have changed then.

The expected level of student achievement in the subject ought to be clearly articulated. First of all, we must teach our students what these issues are. We must let them become aware of the future trends and what the appropriate approaches will be. (Andrew Chan – Marketing)

This quotation serves to introduce the first of the principles. Andrew states that "you have to decide what academic purpose and what activities are desirable". The components of curriculum planning, therefore, need to encompass learning outcomes and the teaching activities which will help students achieve those outcomes. A further element in curriculum planning—the need for feedback for evaluation—is included in the principle, and is discussed later in the chapter.

> Planning for teaching includes articulating expected learning outcomes, selecting learning activities and seeking feedback for evaluation from students, as well as determining content.

There are, therefore, four elements to be considered in planning:

- content,
- learning outcomes,
- learning activities, and
- feedback for evaluation.

The Breadth and Depth of Learning Outcomes

The desired learning outcomes go beyond content-centred ones to include consideration of the intellectual capabilities which need to be addressed. Graduates need more than a knowledge of their discipline. The following quotation shows that course planning in physics recognizes a need for creativity and flexibility. There are other examples of how curricula are designed to encourage the development of other capabilities in the following chapter.

To train students to be creative and flexible, we have introduced a new component in most of our courses, that is, making students read journal papers and present their findings. Students find this component the hardest.... We have to persuade and push them to try harder. However, it is easier said than done. For the bright ones, we have to push them to stretch themselves, whereas the less bright, we have to take them by their hands and walk through the process with them. It is very time-consuming. (Chu Ming Chung – Physics)

The necessary outcomes of a programme might be specified as knowledge of particular content areas together with a set of core competencies. If the programme is to be successful, its planning needs to identify which competencies are necessary and determine how they are to be nurtured in identified courses.

> Students have to acquire core competencies such as the ability to make decisions; the ability to prioritize, to extrapolate the risky from the less risky; and the ability to communicate. (Leung Sing Fai – Clinical Oncology)

Developing these capabilities occurs in courses which make intellectual demands upon students. Qualities like critical thinking develop through students engaging in analytical debate about key topics. As a result, well-planned courses can be demanding.

Student-Centred Planning

Another planning principle was that the exemplary teachers took a student-centred perspective in planning their courses. The future requirements of students were anticipated and consideration given to their lifelong learning needs.

> When planning courses it is necessary to anticipate the needs of the students.

Students' future career needs were anticipated. The following quotation indicates how this was applied in education. Theory was meshed with practice so that students would appreciate the relevance of the course.

> I will select teaching theory that is practical to my students' everyday teaching life. In addition to teaching plain theory, I apply examples of teaching experiences in high schools. I would like to integrate theory with teaching experiences. To facilitate better understanding, I also arrange the class venue like a real classroom setting. (Patrick Lau – Educational Psychology)

Course planning could look beyond the end of a course to consider lifelong learning needs. Most commonly this was through ensuring that courses played a part in developing the intellectual capabilities needed for lifelong learning, as indicated above. In the quotation below, students are referred to readings which will help them in the future:

> Most of my students are part-time students and they hold positions such as high school principals or teachers. They are very busy and seldom have time to read books. In this connection, I think reference materials are important for them. Reference materials are prepared to facilitate students' lifelong learning. Although they may not review the reference materials immediately, well-prepared materials

may help them in the long run. Because of the above reason, I put a lot of effort into the preparation of reference materials. (John Chi Kin Lee – Curriculum and Instruction)

Programme and Course Level Planning

This section looks at how the principles of planning are applied at programme and course level. The following section considers the planning of individual lessons.

The first quotation shows the importance of anticipating student needs. What is included in courses is what students will need in the future.

> We have students in our minds when designing courses: What will students want to learn? Why are these skills and ideas useful for them in the future? The courses are primarily designed for students. We want to educate them so that they can go out to the real world and work with the tools and techniques they have learnt. From time to time, we also launch very specific, focused areas, and this always gauges the demand of the students. (Fan Jianqing – Statistics)

The following quotation illustrates both the principle of student-centred planning and the use of all four of the elements of curriculum design. Feedback is sought on desired learning outcomes in the form of competencies to be developed. Content is addressed through an update on the literature and trends in marketing. Learning activities are addressed through reference to experience and examining international practice.

> I collect such useful information by several means: I'll ask them to fill in a questionnaire "What do you expect to learn in the course?" Then I'll figure out what kinds of competencies are required of them from the real world. From time to time, I'll find out from alumni and business people what kinds of people are currently needed in their fields, and I will aim at developing such competencies in my students. Preceding that, I have to constantly update my literature understanding before designing the curriculum content. Therefore, the final curriculum content is tailored to meet current requirements and future trends alongside the understanding of prevailing issues in the academic world. I will integrate all this information and share with my students.
>
> Course design is taken very seriously and carefully. At a programme level, the programme directors are responsible for identifying or selecting the most relevant courses. We ask ourselves:
> - What are the objectives of the programme?
> - What do we expect the graduates to achieve when they have completed the programme?
> - What is required in the world and what are the future trends?

We will know what key areas are involved. For example, I am teaching marketing and I will focus on the needs and the trend in the arena of marketing.

What is required of each of the different function areas in business education? To achieve this, you have to select the content, and appropriate persons for the design and teaching of the course. Previous experience in teaching that particular subject is an important source of reference. We'll look into international practices for teaching approaches and materials. (Andrew Chan – Marketing)

The following quotation deals with arranging guest speakers. This can be interpreted as both preparing learning activities and introducing variety in content through the contrasting voices. It also shows the value of student feedback—this time from the look in their eyes.

It's hard work to prepare for a new curriculum and to arrange a series of guest speakers. But I can tell from students' eyes that they really enjoyed it and were deeply moved. They were thankful for all these efforts: different input from different people with different voices. (Lo Wai Luen – Chinese Literature)

Planning Lessons

Planning lessons is also important. Francis Chan explained the need to think carefully about how to explain content clearly so that it will be understood. He also discussed the need to have a variety of learning activities as students' concentration span is exceeded if an activity, and particularly lecturing, goes on for too long.

First of all, good preparation is required in my part for each class. Without preparation, my teaching may become disorganized and confusing. I'll challenge myself, "How can I explain the complex and difficult knowledge in the simplest ways?"

If I can make a layman understand my teaching, that's a real success. Students may just be a bit better than laymen. So, that's a real challenge. Secondly, how can I induce their interest in learning and consolidate their memory? Thirdly, time span in explaining should not be too long. I'll make sure that my tutorial won't last longer than 30 minutes; that's the limit for students' time span for concentration. I pay attention to students' gestures. If they look as if they are about to drop off, I'll give a little recess, let them go to the restroom, or just joke with them for a bit to refresh them. (Francis Chan – Medicine and Therapeutics)

Adaptability in Class

The next quotation reiterates the need for preparation. Exemplary teachers go into a lesson with a carefully prepared plan of what they are going to do. They also recognize the need to adapt their plan depending on student reactions.

Every lesson has a predetermined structure. In other words, it needs to be prepared. But you need to be flexible within that structure when you're teaching a lesson; have the flexibility to cater for student needs or issues that you haven't thought about. It's inevitable and you'll have to deal with those when they come up. So prepare very carefully, and structure what you expect students to get out of the lesson, then be prepared to move along with that as you go on.

It can be done in many ways. I'd quite often, within a lesson, decide to do something when I walk in the door, or after half an hour of the lesson if something is not working, or if I think there is a better way to do it. I work on the "three-yawn rule", if I see three yawns in a short period of time in a class, I'll do something else. I'll switch to an activity or I'll get the students involved in another way. It's my responsibility to keep them interested and to keep them coming. If they don't, it's more an indication of me failing. You can't win them all, but I try to stick to that rule if I can. I just have a "grab-bag" of ways of teaching that you can pull out and use, this for this occasion or that for that occasion, depending on the students. (Allan Walker – Educational Administration)

Teachers should make a detailed plan of each lesson, including learning activities, but then be prepared to flexibly adapt the plan in the light of students' responses.

Experienced teachers watch their students and learn to interpret their reactions. Facial expressions can indicate when something is not understood. Boredom or drifting off show that the teacher has talked for long enough and it is time for interaction.

My perception is teachers generally talk too much. You can tell somebody's puzzled by the way they look. And you can tell if somebody is not paying attention, often because I'm talking too much. You can tell that somebody is subtly drifting off; that's the time to ask questions, to get them moving and to keep them in. It's monitoring what's going on really. I try and make it so that I don't talk more than 50–60% of the time at most. The rest of the time is students'. Whenever I teach, I have all these questions I'm going to ask them about. (Gordon Mathews – Anthropology)

Different teachers had somewhat different ways of anticipating and reacting to students in class. There were variations in the way they described how to encourage interaction.

Sometimes I'll ask them whether they understand the materials. They will be in deep silence. I have to joke, "Who doesn't have a question raise your hands!" They'll laugh and become more open. Students just do not want to speak up and you have to try everything. You have to gauge directly to see if they understand the material. Sometimes, directly you can see it on their faces. You don't get it directly because they don't want to appear to be too smart; nor do they want to appear to be stupid either. (Soung Liew – Information Engineering)

The need for adaptability in class is very graphically illustrated by the following analogy:

> Teaching is just like a dance. You need to closely look and feel your partner in the dance, if their steps are confused, if they follow the music. If you know that your partner is a bit clumsy, you will need to adjust and help your partner. Skip those difficult fancy steps until your partner reaches a certain level. There are enough lessons for you to gradually guide them and for them to catch up. They can then dance beautifully. Be patient and let them learn gradually. If they cannot dance well, I have to check on my part. (Andrew Chan – Marketing)

Feedback for Improvement

Another important part of course planning is the use of feedback. Excellent teachers recognize that there are always ways in which a course can be improved. Initial plans are carefully made and then fine-tuned in the light of student feedback. This feedback for evaluation comes from a variety of sources including direct conversation with students, information from Teaching Assistants (TAs) and course evaluation questionnaires.

> Generally speaking, students are extremely important in helping shape what a class should cover. And so I listen a great deal to what I am told in the course of the class and what the TA tells me. So they have a fundamental role in telling me how I should proceed. For example, I'd always ask students at the end of a course, "Which of these books do you most like? Which do you least like? Which would you not want to use next year?"

> Course evaluations are helpful to see what things didn't work. In my course evaluations, what is going up is how much and how hard students worked and those are incredibly high. That's good in that people are really working. They know what to expect. (Gordon Mathews – Anthropology)

Four-Element Planning Model

In planning for teaching the excellent teachers made use of a four-element curriculum development model. These four elements are:
- learning outcomes;
- content;
- learning activities; and
- feedback for evaluation.

23

There was no specific order in which the elements were followed. Notice, for example, that, in one of the quotations from Andrew Chan, obtaining feedback is the first step in developing a new programme, whereas in the above quotation from Gordon Mathews, feedback was obtained at the end of a course.

The four elements of the curriculum planning model are, therefore, best shown as all capable of leading to, or influencing, each other. A diagrammatic version of the curriculum development model is shown below. The model is similar to the interactive model of curriculum development (see e.g., Brady, 1990), except with some differences in the four elements.

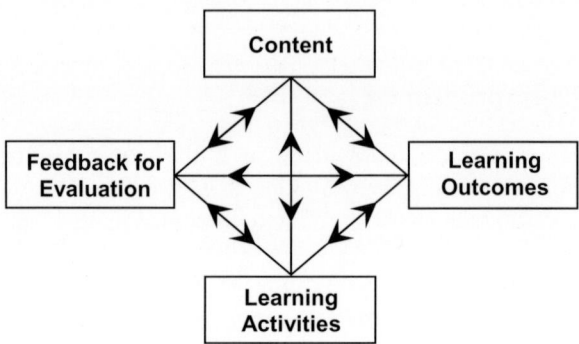

Figure 3.1. Four-Element Planning Model

Chapter 4

What is Taught

The exemplary teachers came from each of the seven faculties at CUHK. Within each faculty the teachers were from various departments. As CUHK is a comprehensive university, the excellent teachers, therefore, came from a diverse range of disciplines.

Examining the interview transcripts on the topic of content might then be expected to result in diversity along disciplinary lines rather than the commonalities sought through the approach to grounded qualitative data analysis. Becher (1989) has argued that universities consist of academic tribes owing primary allegiance to their discipline.

What is taught in anthropology is clearly different to what is included in the electronic engineering curriculum. Nevertheless, it was possible to see some common principles in how content was selected. When planning what was taught there were some general principles which the excellent teachers followed, which are derived in this chapter.

Fundamental Concepts

The most important principle was avoiding a mass of detail in favour of concentrating upon key concepts. Students cannot possibly remember all the detail in a topic area now that we are in an era of information explosion, so why try to cover everything? As long as the principles are understood, the detail can be looked up when, or if, it is needed.

> One could have taught them all the content which will be examined. But for me, this is confusing the means with the ends. My teaching is not content-driven. I teach how to solve problems. Some students will panic after my class, "When teaching lymphatic lumps, you've only taught two ways of solving the lymphatic problems. But there are 14 different types and you haven't even mentioned them! What can we do if they come up in exams?"
>
> I'll explain to them that they can find the details of the 14 types in the textbooks, which will have much better detail than I can ever cover in a lesson. For me to repeat these facts in class is meaningless. The specific details of the 14 types are not necessary unless they become specialists in this field. The most important at this stage is for them to be able to distinguish the serious from the not-serious cases, and what further steps need to be taken to help the patient. It is good if you can remember, say, type 1 has such and such characteristics and patients are usually between 24 to 48 years old.… But the other aspects are more important. (Gregory Cheng – Medicine and Therapeutics)

The importance of concentrating upon fundamental concepts was stated by 15 of the 18 interviewees. Although the disciplines were diverse there was recognition that there were inherent fundamental concepts. Chu Ming Chung, for example, talked of foundation knowledge in physics:

> This requires a crucial foundation for acquiring advance knowledge. In physics, the four fundamental mechanics theories and mathematical knowledge are prerequisites. (Chu Ming Chung – Physics)

Even a subject as recent and rapidly changing as computer engineering had fundamental concepts. It could be argued that it is even more important to concentrate upon key concepts in dynamic subjects since detailed information becomes outdated so quickly.

> In the field of engineering, the fundamental knowledge is most important, such as maths and programming. Technology advances rapidly while the fundamental knowledge remains unchanged. For example, Java has been popular for a while. Then a few months ago, Microsoft announced that they were not going to support Java anymore. That's why we teach the fundamentals so that students can establish a solid foundation and be able to adapt and learn new things more easily. (John Lui – Computer Science and Engineering)

Fan Jianqing used a variation on the metaphor of seeing the wood from the trees to show why it is important to concentrate upon key concepts. This quotation also introduces the idea of giving students a conceptual map to help understanding. Seeing where a concept fits into an overall picture helps in reaching an understanding of it.

> I believe that as statisticians, students need to understand some concepts before they are presented with some key arguments. It is like giving them a whole picture of the landscape of the jungle before going into details with a particular tree so that they won't get lost in the jungle right at a start. (Fan Jianqing – Statistics)

Making Fundamental Concepts Explicit

The quotation below reiterates the principle of concentrating on important points rather than detail. It also takes further the importance of making sure students know what they are. Lectures normally include key concepts, but also contain other material such as illustrations, amplifications and examples. Unless the material is explicitly structured, students often find it difficult to distinguish the principles from the remainder. The quotation serves to introduce the first principle in this chapter.

> Whenever you copy from me, you are simply passing stuff from your ears, through your spine, then your hands, and excrete through your pen! It will not enter into your brain that way. On the contrary, I do not allow you to copy, and you have to force yourselves to think and then remember. You can't possibly

remember all that I've taught you in that hour. You need to end up by remembering the important things that I've taught and forget the trivial details. If you can only remember three main points in the whole lesson that's good enough. Not to worry if you have forgotten the stuff that is secondary since you have so many other important things to remember. It's a misperception that you can revisit and learn from the notes that you've mindlessly copied and dictated during lessons. My past experience tells me that you will not have a clue what you've scribbled down. You won't be able to extrapolate the important points.

Simple messages are easier to understand and remember. Conveying messages in a simple and clear manner does require skills. At the start of each class, I will state very clearly the learning objectives, "I want you to learn four things in the following half hour, they are ..." At the end of each class, I will ask, "What is the 'take-home' message from this lesson?" Then I'll reemphasize, "Among the four things we've learnt, if you can't remember them all, you must however not forget this very aspect as it is crucial for being a good doctor." (Francis Chan – Medicine and Therapeutics)

> Teachers should concentrate on teaching key concepts, rather than detail, and make the fundamental points explicit.

An alternative way of making the fundamental points explicit is providing a road map of the lesson:

What I've learnt from this guy is: at the beginning of each lesson—it's so basic when you think about it but so many people don't do it—he told us what the lesson is about and what you are going to achieve. It's so simple when I say it but it was almost foreign to me. So right from the beginning of that lesson, I knew what I was doing and I knew what was expected. (Allan Walker – Educational Administration)

Relevance

Another principle in selecting content is to ensure that students perceive that the material has some relevance. When learning theory is seen as a purely abstract exercise, it can be perceived as little more than an assignment undertaken because it might come up in the examination. However, if relevance is established students can see why the concept is important, and thus find it easier to understand what has become a more real phenomenon.

> Teachers should select content which students can perceive as relevant and show how it is relevant.

Relevance was established in several different ways. The first example shows how theory can be shown to be relevant through real life examples:

> Let me give a very simple statistics example—hypothesis testing. It is a little bit dry and people don't understand it very well. I will explain it using a real life situation such as drugs use in health service. Doctors may not be able to judge if certain drugs are effective or not since there are variations in usage among the health care population in which some doctors will prescribe them to patients and some don't. Results show that there are small differences. How do we know if the differences are by chance, or intrinsically, one drug is better than the other? This is an elementary enough example. But you can make it even more elementary. People think that they can tell the difference between Coke and Pepsi. So I bring the drinks in without labels and ask them to taste and tell me which is which. If 50% of the answer is correct, it is quite obvious that they guess it right by chance. What about 55% and more? The question then is, where is the cut-off point that we can confidently say that you have the ability to differentiate between Coke and Pepsi?
>
> So these are very simple, concrete real life examples to stimulate students' interest in learning and make important concepts more easily understood. After that, we can go into more detailed, abstract and complicated examples. (Fan Jianqing – Statistics)

Another way of establishing relevance is to make use of examples from current affairs. Teachers using this strategy have to keep abreast of the news:

> Keep asking them questions. Those are not technical questions that appear in textbooks. They are questions that emphasize everyday application. This is particularly important in business…. I myself have to watch the news twice a day and read a couple of newspapers to keep up to date with events which can be applied in management and then share them with students. (Gordon Cheung – Management)

A final method is through establishing local relevance. This is a particularly important approach as textbooks often originate overseas, usually from Western countries. Examples given in them can often appear of little relevance to the Hong Kong context.

> Too often, students don't think about their currency within their own context. For example, when we talk about student-centred learning, leadership, I don't just give them theories that have been developed in the United States or Australia. I will talk to students about them, and then we will go through them and see if they hold here…. What I teach has to be relevant to the students. I have to make sure that the theoretical perspectives relate to their practice and help them to apply that, try to understand what they are doing through application. To do so you've got to know what's going on in your field and the community as well. So, I am teaching people from schools or from bureaucracy, I have to know what happens in schools and the policies. I have to understand what people are

thinking, making sense of their job. If I don't understand that, it's difficult for me to make sense of what I'm teaching to them. So I've got to know what happens in Hong Kong classrooms. (Allan Walker – Educational Administration)

Fifteen of the 18 interviewees had some mention of content relevance in their transcript. Establishing the relevance of content is also seen as one of the ways of motivating students to learn it. This is one of the strategies introduced in Chapter 6, which is on the topic of motivating students.

Learning to Learn

In selecting what to teach the excellent teachers were aware of the elements of course planning dealt with in the previous chapter. What is taught is not just a matter of covering the content appropriate for a particular topic, but the desired learning outcomes also have to be considered. Gordon Mathews justifies this conclusion through the nature of his discipline, which is anthropology:

> Anthropology is a discipline designed to make people think about their lives. My teaching is to teach people how to think and make them question everything around them. Anthropology specifically has to do with the ways in which we are moulded socially and culturally by our worlds. For instance, people think that grades are measures of intelligence. Not necessarily. Grades can be seen as ways society filters people into social classes. So what I am trying to teach is ways in which people can question their social moulding. (Gordon Mathews – Anthropology)

Perhaps the most important learning outcome is that students learn how to learn for themselves. When they graduate there will be many new topics they will need to learn, so it is important that their university education develops their capacity to do so. Chan Hung Kan shows how to do this through requiring students to discover the origin of words from first principles. Requiring students to work out problems, rather than just telling them the solutions, provides a training in thinking ability:

> When I am teaching philology, we will encounter some problems investigating the origin of words. For example, 打尖 (da2jim1) means jumping the queue. But how does the second character come to replace the original complicated character which very few people know how to write out? Sometimes, the origin of some words is even more difficult to trace and different scholars have different opinions. How do we deal with this? I teach students to analyse from the structure, sound and meaning of the word. We also need to know its original usage. Never stick with the first opinion and not be able to debate and discuss its legitimacy. They need to read through a lot of references about the historical development of the sound and the written form of a word before forming a sensible judgment. We may have to contrast the present phonological system with the classical one. Students need to spend a lot of time doing exercises such as these so as to strengthen their thinking ability. (Chan Hung Kan – Chinese Language)

> What is taught should take into account students' need to develop the ability to learn for themselves. Self-managed learning ability can be nurtured through student-centred approaches to teaching.

Developing self-learning ability requires the teacher to be a guide or facilitator rather than a didactic lecturer.

> I've become more open to my students, let them develop their independent thinking through my teaching and guidance. I would tell them, "These are the authors and their backgrounds. Can you put your feet into their shoes and enter into their lives through their writings, how they lived in their times?" (Lo Wai Luen – Chinese Literature)

Developing the capacity to be a self-managed learner comes through student-centred approaches to teaching. These can require students to engage in highly active forms of learning, which many would have had little experience of at school. In most cases students see the value in these forms of learning and eventually prefer them. There is little truth in the widespread perceptions that Hong Kong students prefer passive forms of learning.

> In the past couple of years, I emphasize more the enhancement of self-learning and arousing interest in students. For instance, we organize a case competition within the faculty. About 10 teams of roughly 100 students participate each year. We'll think of ways which make the competition a fun event. They are given a case on Friday and they have to present their analysis the next day. They will have to burn the midnight oil that night. They all moan but are fully charged and enjoy the whole event to the full, and they ask for more similar events. These kinds of activities are effective in motivating self-learning. (Gordon Cheung – Management)

The process of introducing changes to ways of thinking and learning needs to be gradual. Those who are dropped in at the deep end are more likely to sink than swim. Lessons need to be given at the shallow end until confidence develops.

> So, my teaching will move from a more structured approach at the beginning to a more open-ended one towards the end; the teacher will move away from readily providing answers to giving no concrete answers eventually. This is exactly what the real world is: no definite answers for questions. At the start, they will gain confidence from "getting the answers right". This confidence is important to enable them to gradually discover that there are no absolute concrete answers, but rather a logic or framework of thinking, based upon which they can formulate their viewpoints, judgments and predictions. Learning is about developing their own thinking rather than finding model answers. (Andrew Chan – Marketing)

Conflicting Theories

The quotation above also serves to introduce the importance of exposing students to conflicting theories. Many students enter university in Hong Kong with unsophisticated epistemological beliefs (Kember, 2001). They have spent much of their time at school being prepared for examinations which largely consist of questions with just one correct answer. Not surprisingly they expect problems to be well-defined, and so are poorly equipped to deal with conflicting theories.

Developing intellectual qualities, such as critical or creative thinking, can only happen if more reflective epistemological beliefs are developed so that students are able to make evaluative judgements on ill-defined issues (King & Kitchener, 1994). These more sophisticated epistemological beliefs develop through gradually increasing exposure to conflicting theories. The ability to make judgements on competing theories is integral to self-managed learning.

> I teach astrophysics. I want my students to know that there are plenty of new discoveries in recent years, some of which are beyond the scientists' imagination in the past. Therefore, to keep your mind open and accept new things is vital. Our knowledge is expanding so much that it is impossible for us to catch up with all the new scientific discoveries of today. We should have the confidence that we have the ability to learn new things by ourselves. (Chu Ming Chung – Physics)

The exemplary teachers recognized that they should be helping students develop the ability to evaluate evidence and make judgements. These abilities could be developed through weighing conflicting theories in the particular subject area.

> In every subject, there are always some conflicting opinions or theories which may be confusing at times. Good teaching should be able to show a good system to analyse them and enable students to form their own sound judgments. For example, when teaching the origin of Chinese characters, there is a serious debate as to whether it began three thousand years ago (as the traditional view claims) or seven thousand years ago. My teaching last year and this year differs as there are now more archaeological finds which suggest that it could easily differ by a couple of thousands years. (Chan Hung Kan – Chinese Language)

Thinking processes developed through discipline-based learning equip students to make sound judgements in other areas.

> There is plenty of room for discussion and no standard answer to these questions. That is why journalism is so exciting and will inspire those who are interested. Such a process of thinking, debating and investigating is valuable for students who are eager to learn and apply what they have learned in journalism to other personal decision-making. (Kenneth Leung – Journalism)

Exposure to conflicting theories seemed to be important in a variety of disciplines. There are those who believe that, particularly at lower levels, disciplines such as science and engineering are relatively factual. The quotations from physics above and engineering below show that the excellent teachers did not believe this.

> Students need the ability to think independently in an "out of box" way. Not just "problem set, solve the problem, compute the answers" which is a very typical way for engineering students. In real life, it is useful but not the most useful. What is important is to think independently, being able to solve an open-ended problem, finding answers by doing research, being able to articulate the trade-offs of different answers and weigh their pluses and minuses. In engineering, there are seldom right or wrong answers. There are always multiple possible answers. You have to weigh what is the trade-off of different solutions and try the best one for that particular situation. So, being able to adapt to the environment and find solutions in a very flexible way is important. That comes with communication skills. (Soung Liew – Information Engineering)

Capabilities

The previous chapter noted that course planning should consider desired learning outcomes. Major facets of these are the types of capabilities graduates will need. The excellent teachers saw these capabilities as being something their courses should develop. They were aware of what capabilities were needed by graduates of their discipline, or in the case of professional courses, by professionals in the field. They recognized that these capabilities should develop through the teaching of discipline-based knowledge, rather than being taught independently as a generic skill. In this way the capabilities were appropriate for the profession or discipline. No less than 16 of the 18 exemplary teachers dealt with the need for developing graduate capabilities when interviewed.

Recognizing and resolving conflicting theories is a complement or prerequisite to the development of capabilities. This section and the previous one, therefore, lead to a joint principle.

> Exposing students to conflicting theories helps develop more sophisticated beliefs about knowledge, and this facilitates the development of important graduate capabilities.

In business, the analytical power to handle ill-defined problems was described as "business sense":

> A lot of students do not have a business sense. For instance, some students will hand in their projects and proposals without mentioning money. I don't mean to be "money-minded" but all business proposals need to have sound budgeting. That's a real problem. The main difference between business students and students from other faculties is precisely this "business sense".

> Business students need to acquire good "business sense" to form an important basis for their analytical powers. They need to analyse a problem with a comprehensive approach rather than a narrow approach. The lack of business sense and a comprehensive approach to problems are not unique to students reading business in CU; it's universal. In fact, CU is doing better because our courses are integrated ones. (Gordon Cheung – Management)

In medicine diagnostic skills were seen as more important than textbook knowledge:

> First, you have to put yourself into patients' shoes; then use your professional knowledge to solve their problems. Patients usually come with some very vague complaints, such as, "I have headache, or I have stomach ache". You'll need to know how to ask questions and what kinds of examinations are needed. It's a doctor's responsibility to judge if their complaints are serious or not and treat them accordingly. Students tend to approach problems by memorizing textbook knowledge, the 40 pages about headache, for example. Instead, they should start from understanding the patient's situation, how they can ask the few questions so as to tease out that the symptoms are not related to the first ten cases, nor the last ten cases recorded in the books, and be left with only two possibilities, for instance. (Gregory Cheng – Medicine and Therapeutics)

Engineers need communication skills and, perhaps surprisingly, Soung Liew saw them as more important than computational skills:

> Students nowadays do lack communication skills. Compared to students in the Western world, Hong Kong students are weaker in presenting their ideas. In the real world, it is very important to be able to articulate yourself. U.S. students articulate very well in presentations. Even if they have inferior solutions, they can talk their way out. In the real world, it is very important to articulate verbally, in speech and in writing.... That's what troubles me the most. As an engineering teacher, I end up being an English teacher a lot of the time! Students may not realize that. I learned from real experience that English is more important than calculus skills in the engineering field, for example. I can say all of the above because I have obtained real life experience in a company. (Soung Liew – Information Engineering)

It wasn't just those in professional programmes who needed graduate capabilities. Science students also needed communication skills:

> Moreover, science students tend to overlook the importance of acquiring communication skills which include the ability to read books and journal papers, and the ability to discuss and question. (Chu Ming Chung – Physics)

Chapter 5

How it is Taught

Building Relationships with Students

Building a relationship with their students was a prerequisite to engaging in teaching. All interviewees accepted that they needed to make positive steps towards developing relationships. The respect shown to teachers meant that the teacher had to make the first step.

The way the exemplary teachers teach includes discussion with their students. It is hard to engage in discussion with someone you do not know. Developing a relationship is also a motivational strategy. Students respond to those they know and trust.

> By projecting ourselves as genuine teachers, with empathy, we can build up a trustful relationship with students. This relationship is a key factor for enhancing the motivation of students. I would like students to have self-motivation. (Patrick Lau – Educational Psychology).

According to Confucian tradition great respect was shown to scholars and teachers (Wu, 1996). There has been some tendency for this tradition to be maintained, in the school sector at least, so that teachers have a superior and even authoritarian reputation (Lee, 1996). As class sizes in Hong Kong schools are normally large, maintaining this hierarchical relationship between teachers and pupils can be a way to reinforce discipline (Cheung & Lau, 1985).

I. T. Ho (2001) though has argued that this traditional view of teacher–student relationships is an oversimplification. Her research suggested that while Hong Kong classrooms may have a more formal atmosphere than those in the West, school teachers were more likely to develop relationships with students outside class hours. There will be further discussion of this issue in Chapter 9. The quotation below suggests that in universities nowadays the relationships between teachers and students can be on a more equal footing, especially if the teacher takes the trouble to try to encourage the development of closer ties:

> The relationship between teachers and students in Chinese society is usually hierarchical. Nowadays, young people are different from those in the old days. They expect a friendship-type of relationship between their teachers and themselves. Teachers have to adjust their attitude. Both teachers and students should communicate in a mutually acceptable attitude and should understand each other. (John Chi Kin Lee – Curriculum and Instruction)

The quotation below shows that a relationship can be developed through showing a light-hearted side to students to relax any preconceived barriers. Being available outside class hours is important:

> Students think that I'm easy to approach. I joke with them and they feel that they can approach me whenever they come across difficulties in their learning. They can approach me not just during lectures, tutorials or consultation hours, but also after class and they can request an extra lesson if need be. They know that if they are willing to learn, the door is always open, I'm more than happy to teach them. (Gregory Cheng – Medicine and Therapeutics)

These last two quotations are possibly an indication of I. T. Ho's (2001) suggestion that Chinese teachers may be more willing than their Western counterparts to engage with students in out-of-class time. Patrick Lau liked to interact with students over lunch and also went camping with them:

> I like to interact with students during lunch. We can chat about all sorts of things and brainstorm. I recalled that my professors brainstormed with students during my college years. I learned lots of things while chatting with professors.
>
> I spent lots of time in student interaction. Last year, I went camping with officers of the students' association. They started the discussion in criticism. I suggested they start the discussion by showing their appreciation of each group member. I felt there were lots of interpersonal exchanges and the atmosphere was good. I felt that I was younger. I feel that it is worthwhile to spend time in interactive activities. (Patrick Lau – Educational Psychology)

Encouraging communication is an integral part of developing a relationship. Face-to-face communication was seen as the most common medium, and probably the more effective way of establishing an initial rapport. The web can also play a useful role though:

> I emphasize communications with students, particularly communications outside classroom teaching. In recent years, I have created a web forum for each class so that students can post questions whenever they need and wherever they are. And I'll respond as soon as possible. The forums are monitored several times a day, seven days a week. Meanwhile, I equally encourage students to come to me personally to ask questions and have face-to-face interaction. (Chu Ming Chung – Physics)

Getting to Know Students

To build a relationship with students it is necessary to get to know them as individuals. The first step in doing so is to learn their names:

> One technique that I use to break the ice and gradually warm students up for active learning is to remember students' names. In a group of 15 students, they will introduce their names which are impossible for me to remember them all

instantly. So I'll joke with them, "I will only call on the ones whose names are easy to remember." They'll start laughing. "Those who have got easy names, if you don't want me to call on you all the time, you had better give me other fellow students' names after I have asked the question." Students tend to do that without much problem. They quite enjoy calling each others' names and eventually everybody has a chance to participate. Gradually, I can remember and call them by their names, and they really appreciate that. Their participation increases and they'll pay more attention and think more carefully consequently. (Francis Chan – Medicine and Therapeutics)

> Good teachers develop a relationship with their students by getting to know them as individuals.

Getting to know part-time students can be particularly important as fitting in part-time study alongside a full-time job is very demanding. As part-time students are commonly working in the profession or discipline they are studying, it is also necessary to get to know what they do at work so that the course can relate more closely to them. If a relationship is established, conversations with students can then become an important source of feedback for curriculum improvement. This forms one channel for the feedback loop dealt with in Chapter 3.

We teach a lot of part-time classes. Students work from nine to seven. They are tired when they go to the class. If you can't arouse their interest, they will be "dead". To stimulate their interest is basic but challenging. You have to find out who your students are, their concerns and what motivates them.

Constantly, your students are offering suggestions to improve your teaching. To resist appropriate changes is an attitudinal problem. If you are open-minded, you can make relevant improvements. Not all suggestions are reasonable. In some cases, you can modify and improve better than students suggest. (Andrew Chan – Marketing)

Engaging Students in Discussion

The excellent teachers were not didactic. They recognized that student learning is the important outcome of the educational process, and so adopted practices which facilitated learning. Sixteen of the 18 transcripts contained a description of discussion in class. Teaching, therefore, involves interaction with students. The excellent teachers have developed ways of promoting discussion with students.

I prefer to teach in an interactive "question and answer" format. It is recognized in medical training that the lecture style of teaching is the least effective while direct interaction is considered the most effective. Prolonged interaction is preferred to allow students to review real cases and examples. We don't have that much one-way lecturing. If we do, it won't last longer than 30–40 minutes, whereas a continuous Q and A tutorial session can last for an hour and a half. (Leung Sing Fai – Clinical Oncology)

The discussion was not confined to that between the teacher and students. Discussion among students is also of value, so the teachers prompt their students to discuss ideas and concepts among themselves.

Another important nature of learning is companionship. I always tell my students that learning among fellow students is essential. When they are together, they shouldn't just chit-chat. They should find time to discuss and debate among themselves. A Chinese saying goes: Studying alone without company restricts learning to narrowness (獨學而無友則孤陋而寡聞). Many discoveries are made through debate and discussion among peers, challenging and stimulating each other. (Chan Hung Kan – Chinese Language)

A vital constituent of excellent teaching is interaction in class between the teachers and their students, and the promotion of discussion among students.

Ways of Promoting Discussion

There are strategies for encouraging interaction and discussion. There are those who are convinced that Hong Kong students are passive and reluctant to speak out in class. Many might seem quiet at first, which is hardly surprising if they have received years of conditioning at school to be passive receivers. However, the exemplary teachers have ways of overcoming any reluctance to engage in class discussion.

The following quotation illustrates two of these. The first is for initial discussions to be between small groups of students. Once a group view has been formulated students become keen for the group's opinions to be presented to the class. A spokesperson can then talk on behalf of the group. The other strategy was that of giving students the questions in advance. With time to formulate an answer they are more prepared to speak out.

You have to encourage them to speak more. Give them questions ahead of time and ask them to think about it in a small group. Usually they will respond as a group. They will say, "Our group believes this or that…" as they are less likely to say "I believe this or that…" If you give them preparation time, usually they are pretty good about it. Normally I give them a question to think about and ask them to respond a little bit later, after the break, or the next day or something like that. Usually I find them OK if you do that. (David Ahlstrom – Management)

Another technique is to base the discussion around published papers or set readings. It then needs intelligent questioning from the teacher to draw out student responses.

In seminars, we will discuss some newly published papers and analyse the strength and the weaknesses or limitations of the study, and whether the conclusion is credible. Most importantly, I'll ask them, "If you come across a similar case, will you adopt the new treatment or will you prefer the old? Is the new treatment method supported by adequate evidence? Or would you rather wait and see?"

This is to train them to think. Rather than taking others' published findings as absolute, particularly when medical knowledge advances so rapidly, and unestablished findings or misleading medical information can be found so easily via the internet and the media, students need to be aware of this as they will be asked by patients. How to explain the situation to patients and to discriminate information that is useful to them is vital. (Gregory Cheng – Medicine and Therapeutics)

The next quotation is a lengthy one because it illustrates several relevant points. It describes a strategy used to promote learning through discussion of ill-defined problems in engineering. This in itself is interesting because there are those who mistakenly contend that discussion has little place in science and engineering because the disciplines are more factual.

The teacher promotes discussion with a light-hearted introduction to promote rapport. The discussion is framed around open contemporary issues relevant to the local engineering industry. The problems are given out in advance so that students are prepared for the discussion. The students are formed into small groups to encourage interaction. Having to deal with ill-defined problems challenges the students' epistemological beliefs, and this helps in the development of critical thinking and self-managed learning.

In Hong Kong, students are reluctant to ask questions. Sometimes you have to tell jokes to warm them up. In one of the courses I teach, I try to conduct discussion sessions once every two weeks. Students are organized into groups of three to five. Before the discussion, I give them some open-ended problems to solve rather than regular homework. These are problems without definite answers which students may need to research beforehand on the web. They are supposed to do it independently.

Come the date of discussion, students will gather together and discuss among themselves. TAs and I will walk around to answer questions, anything that is unclear in their mind. But we will not give out answers. There are no definite answers. One week later, they have to submit a report.... In general, they like it.

It's also more open-ended and less structured. I think it is good for students if they can get together and discuss among themselves. It's more like real life. Lectures are very artificial. You just talk and hope that students can absorb.

Q: What kind of problems do you give out in these discussion sessions?

Practical problems. If a certain company is producing one kind of product, I will ask them to check what kind of product it is. How does it relate to what they have learnt in terms of technical implementation? How do they think the engineers in this company implement this product? What are the advantages and disadvantages? This would arouse their thinking better than just learning a programming language and doing a programming assignment.

Q: How do students respond to that?

If you ask them in the performance evaluation questions, they usually respond favourably. However, I think sometimes students are lost. Engineering students like definite stuff. They do not quite know how to respond to these open-ended questions. In the discussion, a lot of them are positive. Sometimes, they don't know what the question is about. On the other hand, this is what real life is about. When students go out to work, they will face real day-to-day problems. They will be asked to do competitive analysis with competitive products. I think this is a higher level of skills than writing computer software.

The computer software development has been moved to Mainland China. People in China are very good at this at lower cost. Lots of Hong Kong companies have moved their software programming division to China. For architectural designs and customer interactions or marketing, Hong Kong still has an edge in the market. (Soung Liew – Information Engineering)

Teaching Methods

All of the excellent teachers described some method of teaching they employed other than conventional lecturing or holding discussions in seminars or tutorials. The range of principles of good teaching extracted from the interviews shows clearly that the criteria for being selected as an excellent teacher should not be equated to being innovative in teaching—there is much more to it than that. A wide variety of types of teaching were employed, though, and in each case there was a clear rationale for why the particular form had been selected.

This section gives an overview of some of the more popular teaching methods employed. What is important to note is not the method in itself, but the rationale for its use in trying to achieve particular learning outcomes.

Web-Assisted Teaching

Web-assisted teaching has become quite common. Many teachers use it to store information which students can download. The excellent teachers are more interested in its capacity for enhancing communication. In this mode it can be a strategy for building relationships with students and ensuring that teaching features interaction between teacher and students, and among student peers.

> Almost all teachers in the department use the web as a way to post their teaching material for homework and get student feedback in the newsgroups. Students can exchange ideas in the newsgroups although most of the time they ask mundane questions like, what is the due date? ... Still, you get some idea what sort of problem they are facing. Things like the computer going down for five days and they are late for their assignment.... These are important to know. Anyway, a lot of exchange is happening on the web. (Soung Liew – Information Engineering)

The quotation below is a continuation of one cited, in the first section of this chapter, to make the point that communication can be through the web. What is noted here is that some students prefer to interact through a web forum, while others prefer face-to-face discussion. Using a combination of the two makes it easier to reach out to all students.

> Web forum is suitable for shy students who would never ask questions in class nor come to me after class. Interestingly, some of these kids are very active in participating in the forum, questioning and responding. Kids nowadays are accustomed to the subculture of communicating through the internet. They like spending time at night on the web where they express themselves openly.

> Therefore, one of the advantages of a web forum is that you can start getting familiar with students more easily. However, students react differently to the web. Some students might become even less likely to speak up in class since they can express themselves in another channel through the web. Others get familiar with you through the web and participate more actively in class.

> My opinion is that the excessive use of web forums may have a diminishing return in teaching. It is difficult to go in depth through the web in questioning and discussing. Students who are most in need of guidance may not even know what they do not understand and how to phrase their questions. The web doesn't help them much. We pretty much need to talk with them face to face so that we can guess where their problems lie. (Chu Ming Chung – Physics)

Computer Games and Simulations

Teaching methods often do not fit neatly into discrete categories. The one described in the quotation below involves cases of ethical dilemmas incorporated into a computer game, which was posted on the web:

Last summer, I applied for a courseware development grant for $HK50,000. I used it to make improvement in instructional design for a course. I picked out six cases from more than a hundred, which represent different ethical dilemmas. These cases were converted into computer-simulated games. It took quite a long time to do this due to lack of experience and technical know-how. To make an ethical game interesting is extremely difficult. I hired student helpers who were good at playing computer games, versatile in mind and have taken my courses. It took 9–12 months to post the computer games on the web at the end of this semester. We have encountered many problems because this is our first trial. (Kenneth Leung – Journalism)

Contemporary Materials for Professional Application

There was recognition that teaching materials needed to be interesting, up to date and relevant to the local situation, particularly for professional courses. David Ahlstrom is an ardent collector of material which might make teaching more relevant and interesting. His whole office was a forest of books, videos, papers and teaching materials of all kind. He sat on the arm of the sofa all through the interview as this was the only space available, sharing his ideas and experience in teaching, undisturbed by the telephone that kept ringing. The types of materials used ranged from videos to computer simulations:

I bring in materials that I think are relevant and interesting like videos, humorous if possible, or both. Ideally, hands-on experiential learning is the best. But it is difficult to do in class. Therefore, what is a little bit easier sometimes is providing video examples or computer programmes that they can see in action, and better appreciate the business problem at hand. With computer-simulated programmes, they enter some numbers and get some results so that they can compete with each other. There are some strategy games like that. (David Ahlstrom – Management)

Case Studies

Cases are important as a way of exposing students to real life issues, which normally consist of ill-defined problems. Cases can range from simple examples or experiences needing elaboration, to lengthy scenarios. The first example is of the use of examples based on the experience of the teacher in the engineering industry:

For the engineering field, if you want to relate the teaching material to real life, the teacher must have some industrial experience. It would be good if a teacher conducts consultancy in a company or takes leave to go and actually work in the real world, to see what kind of skills are in demand. Otherwise, how can I talk about real life when I don't have real life experience? How can I swim if I don't jump and swim in the pool myself? It's very important to have those experiences. Once you have those experiences, you have a lot of little stories here and there to tell your students. It's good for students to know that in real life, you have this and this problems, and how you can solve them. Students appreciate this knowledge because most of the students have not worked outside and they don't know what kind of skills is required of them. (Soung Liew – Information Engineering)

The next example of using medical cases illustrates the importance of using a good questioning technique with the cases. Putting students into different imaginary scenarios makes them consider the case data in different ways.

In designing courses, I mainly use case studies, real life pathological cases. Instead of a factual knowledge delivery approach, I'll think of many different scenarios and discuss the problem with students. I will always start a course with a case and add variations as I go along so as to induce student thinking from different angles. For instance, a case of stomach bleeding, "If a patient vomits blood in front of you, what will you do?" When an answer is given, I will then progress, "If he has vomited so much that he faints, and your senior is unavailable, what will you do?"

Some light-hearted scenarios are also used: "Today, you have just opened your own practice in City One, Shatin, your first patient comes to you with a stomach ache, what will you do?" They will probably reply, "I'll ask for the history of his complaints, examine his body and take some blood samples".

This is a standard practice in hospital. So, I'll challenge them, "Have you ever been to a private practice? Private practitioners will only spend about three minutes per patient! If you do what is standard in the hospital, it will take up at least half an hour and you probably have a long queue of patients waiting. If you have only three minutes, you can't possibly keep up the standard."

Another scenario is that this patient comes back to you and says, "Your prescription is not effective. If you don't give me something better, I'll go to Dr. Wong next door." What will you do?

I'll give real life scenarios such as these to stimulate students' thinking in a more lively and relaxed atmosphere than a factual presentation of textbook knowledge. The scenario-based questions that I asked are application-oriented. "If a patient comes to you with such and such symptoms, what will you do?" When an answer is given, I will continue asking, "Can you explain why you chose to do that?"

I always remind my students to imagine taking a role of a lawyer, for instance, and look at their own practice since there is no one single absolute approach. Each decision has its advantages and disadvantages. The main thing is about your ability to justify your decision, how you weigh the pros and cons and come up with the final decision. "Imagine that you are a lawyer, how will you question the legitimacy of your treatment? Can you defend your choice of action?" During the process of learning, I will ask a lot of questions, "Why do you choose your treatment?" and "How do you justify your choice?" This enforces students to critically think. Well, I also ask students if they watch ER! (Francis Chan – Medicine and Therapeutics)

The next quotation shows the value in spending time gathering local material to use in cases. This makes the course more interesting and relevant than if cases are taken from overseas.

I have been teaching a course for undergraduates and another for postgraduates on ethics. I am developing some theories and principles in this field. I want to introduce students to dilemma situations or what moral reasoning is. Numerous cases will be used. The book that I have almost finished writing includes approximately 200 cases which I have collected within the last ten years. They are very interesting. This is a casebook on ethical cases. I use cases that students are familiar with such as the bribery case that *Apple Daily* had committed with a policeman. Students certainly have read this in the news. They will find the case familiar and yet new in the sense that they are viewing it from an ethical perspective of how reporters handle such situations and make decisions. This case will help them get familiar with the situation which they may face in future as a reporter or an editor.

Every year I collect different cases for students to undertake case studies. New cases emerge as there are a lot of terrible situations reported in newspapers and magazines. These cases are used to illustrate theories, principles, comparisons between East and West, code of ethics and relevant concepts such as accountability, responsibility, what is good and bad, and so forth. They are not theories living or existing in vacuum. These concepts are observable or even measurable in the Hong Kong context. This will arouse interest in those who are keen to study in this field. (Kenneth Leung – Journalism)

Group Projects

A continuation of the above quotation shows how the cases can be used for group projects. Working in a group means that a more substantial topic can be addressed and helps in developing group work skills. If the project ends in a presentation the remainder of the class learns from the work of each group.

At the beginning, I gave them one individual project and one for group work. Modification has been made as students argued intensively how tough it was. They now only work in a small group and have no individual project. Students usually work overnight for the last two to three weeks of a semester. They will have group discussions and debate their findings. I don't give them any standard answers because in ethics you don't have standard answers, you only have different perspectives. You have to debate and select the one which you think is the most appropriate. Thus, plenty of discussions have been carried out. After the series of debates, they have to write up. I understand that is a tough process. (Kenneth Leung – Journalism)

Student Presentations

This quotation shows a somewhat different way of using student presentations. Instead of the teacher presenting all the material, each student is given responsibility for finding out about a particular section and then presenting that material to the class.

> They have presentations to do as well. You'll give them a topic and they have to prepare to present and then lead discussions afterwards. Most students like that given they have the time. This is done when they have been given some foundation knowledge. We'll encourage them to look up to the most advanced information on the internet. (Gregory Cheng – Medicine and Therapeutics)

Learning Outside the Classroom

Teaching and learning are not confined to the classroom, as some lessons are best learnt through exposure to the real situation during field trips. These visits could be trips overseas.

> I have organized a bigger scale "Study Abroad Programme". After their final exam in May, myself and a few other teachers will bring students to Japan and Singapore for firm visits. Let them see the world outside and they learn beyond the classroom. I've also learnt from the overseas competitions, how other teams analyse certain cases, what comments have been given, what are the strong points that we can imitate from others. (Gordon Cheung – Management)

Variety of Approaches

The excellent teachers do not restrict their teaching approaches to one method, but use a variety of techniques depending on what is being taught.

> I think there should be a main theme. For example, if I am teaching communication, there should be verbal and nonverbal communication. Students may observe the above areas in nonclassroom settings. Eye contact and verbal communication are means of communication.
>
> I tried to let students have a feel about communication. I request some help from students who are fluent orally. I asked a student to explain verbally a selected object, such as a bottle. I then asked other students as an audience to draw a picture about the object. The students spent about five minutes. I allowed the audience to ask questions. After the question and answer session, some audience members started to modify the picture that they have drawn. I let students express their feelings about the whole process. This is a good exercise in a way that students can play opposite roles and respect each role's perspective.

45

I also share teaching experiences with students and demonstrate to them the ways I handle each situation. Sometimes, I ask students to fill in a questionnaire to know more about their psychological state. Videos are used to assist the lecture and enrich the discussion.

All of the above activities are designed to encourage self-reflection. I think self-reflection is crucial in a teacher training programme. A teacher with good reflection skills would review his techniques and knowledge. (Patrick Lau – Educational Psychology)

> Excellent teachers use a variety of teaching methods appropriate to the desired learning outcomes.

Variety in Assessment

Students are assessment-driven, and this must be close to being a universal reality. Rather than bemoaning the fact, the exemplary teachers take care to design appropriate assessment which directed the assessment drive towards the desired learning outcomes. To achieve this goal there needs to be consistency between the learning outcomes included in the curriculum plan and the assessment used to test the achievement of these outcomes.

I have no objection to an assessment-driven learning style. It's a matter of means and ends. We should use the means, assessment, to make student learn better at the end. Assessment is part of the curriculum. We should think carefully about the function of assessment. (John Chi Kin Lee – Curriculum and Instruction)

Examinations were not strongly favoured. The NVivo word search facility was used to search the transcripts for terms like "examinations". Only one of the interviewees described the use of examinations as a major part of the assessment in their course and commented on it in a positive light. To the contrary, there were reservations about examinations.

Unfortunately, we rely on examinations a lot. Examinations are still a substantial part of assessment. The University has a committee on assessment which recommends to teachers that a certain percentage of the grade has to come from examinations. This is very inflexible. I think this is bad practice. … life does not operate in this way. When you graduate and go out to work, you don't have this kind of setting. (Soung Liew – Information Engineering)

The journalism course eschewed examinations in favour of projects. The rationale was that projects are better able to encourage and test the desired learning outcome, which in this case was in-depth analysis.

There is no examination in this subject. I just ask students to do projects. Students have to do some analysis in their projects. Then I can examine whether the analysis is in-depth and if the student is able to identify the problem. All these show how much a student has learnt. Therefore, the grade reflects how much students have learnt, and their analytical ability. (Kenneth Leung – Journalism)

There was also no great enthusiasm for multiple-choice questions. A similar word search found no positive mention of them in any of the transcripts. Given the nature of open semistructured interviews, this does not mean that none of the interviewees used them, but it does suggest that they were hardly a major feature of the assessment employed by the exemplary teachers.

The learning outcomes which need to be developed for business are application, analysis and making judgements on real-life ill-defined problems. Case studies are the main type of assessment as they help develop and test each of these learning outcomes.

My exams are mainly case-based. Seldom do I use multiple-choice or Q and A which is no more than a memory test of rote learning. The very nature of teaching business is that we do case analysis which is applied. Therefore, we assess students' understanding by judging how well they can carry out that application. (Gordon Cheung – Management)

Reflection on Personal Experience

An assessment strategy which has quite wide application is that of asking students to apply theories to their personal situations. The quotation below applies to teachers who were asked to apply theories to reflect upon the situation in their own schools. The outcome is personal development applied directly to the professional role.

A noteworthy side issue of this type of reflection on each individual's situation is that plagiarism is not possible. As each student's situation is unique, another student's work or materials on the internet are not applicable.

I can give you an example of what I want in my assignments. I ask my students to examine organizations using different metaphors, different lenses of understanding it. I don't want them to simply tell me these other ways that we can do certain things. I will say, "The first part of your paper, you've got to give me two or three pages that tell me about the context of your school. I don't mean how many students or buildings you've got, but the feeling of life in your school. Then you apply the theory to that, and you tell me what these metaphors or lenses tell you about your school". (Allan Walker – Educational Administration)

Another example of open assessment which could be related to the individual student situation comes from anthropology. Again the example asks students to make use of theories they have been taught in analysing situations they are familiar with.

> For "Anthropological Theories", the final paper for the people to write was: "Pick any event which is going on in the world today; use five of these theories to explain it." That gets students to think for themselves with any event or any personal interaction. One person described his experience working for a modelling agency, how that could be explained through these different theories. That makes the theories not abstract but directly explicit to people's lives. (Gordon Mathews – Anthropology)

Variety of Assessment

The quotation below shows the use of a variety of interesting assignments and homework, which focus on the outcome of developing reflective thinking. Notice that students can be very imaginative when given open assessment tasks, which turns them from being chores which have to be completed to get a pass, to creative work in which pride is taken.

> Asking students to demonstrate the application of learning theories in term papers is important. Small exercises will be assigned such as the following: "Reflection papers in personal growth in teachers: Ask students to select two articles distributed in class and express their understanding".

> For in-class activities, students can use some topics discussed in class as a base for reflection. Students can be creative in showing their reflection. For example, I asked students to try something they never tried before. The rule of thumb is that the activity must not violate the law.

> As an example of creative activity, some students played the role of picking aluminium cans. They asked those people who have finished playing football to give them the soda cans. The purpose of this activity is to experience the life of various people in society. Students write up the whole process. This is a training method for reflection. The reason for participating in creative activity is to let students know that I don't want students to feel homework is boring. I want students to feel some interest in homework. (Patrick Lau – Educational Psychology)

The main theme which comes out of this examination of assessment practices is that the excellent teachers thought about the learning outcomes which they intended to achieve and tried to devise assessment which would test those outcomes. The process of being tested in the outcomes would mean that students would have to apply them in the assignment so the activity would result in their practising the targeted competency. As the courses taught by the exemplary teachers sought to develop a range of learning outcomes, a wide variety of forms of assessment were used.

Exemplary teachers use a variety of methods of assessment which are valid tests of the planned learning outcomes. These assessment strategies are also consistent with encouraging the development of these outcomes.

Chapter 6

Motivating Students

A very significant point, to be made right at the start, is that there is a chapter on motivating students. All of the interviews refer in some way to the need to motivate students to learn as an integral part of good teaching. The excellent teachers, therefore, accept that it is their responsibility to motivate students.

> Excellent teachers accept that they have a responsibility to motivate their students.

This is not a universal view, however. Many teachers complain that "students no longer come to university interested in learning about my discipline" or "the standard of students is not what it used to be when I was a student". There is no doubt that many of these retrospective views of student behaviour are through rose-tinted glasses which have misted over with time. More significantly, though, they are shifting responsibility for motivation from the teacher to the student. Students are expected to come to university motivated to learn, however dull and boring the classes might be.

The exemplary teachers did not subscribe to this viewpoint. They recognized that they had a role to play in interesting, motivating and inspiring their students towards their expectations.

> Effective teaching refers to arousing students' interests, inspiring them to deep learning, getting them interested in what is being taught and resulting in students having a sense of accomplishment in that learning has taken place within them. In my course, students can apply what they've learnt in situations outside the classroom. One common comment from my student course evaluations is: "I am inspired". (Kenneth Leung – Journalism)

Making Demands on Students

Their expectations were high too. Several interviewees said they knew of teachers whose courses were relatively undemanding. These were courses for which students might expect good grades without being unduly stretched. This description did not apply to their courses though.

> I insist that there is a bottom line. Never lower the standard for students' liking unconditionally or without principles. I know that some teachers will teach easy options, making exams easy to pass or to get high marks, giving extra marks so as to please their students. These are bad examples and they are cheating on their

students. Every year, my students comment that I require too much work. They always moan when I make them dictate the phonetic symbols, for example. However, it is absolutely necessary otherwise they won't be able to use the dictionary. I will insist on the bottom line. (Chan Hung Kan – Chinese Language)

Ratings from students on teacher evaluation questionnaires are a component in the selection process for the exemplary teacher awards. There are those who believe that students choose easy courses, without too much work, and give poor ratings to those who make their courses difficult or demanding. The experiences of the interviewees would seem to suggest that there is little foundation to this belief.

Poor teaching happens when there is no interaction with students. Students also get turned off if the presentation is poor and this is often caused by lack of preparation. Conveying clear concepts to students is a basic requirement of teaching but I did mention before that clear presentation may not be adequate to arouse interest. What students complain about most is courses that are "flat" ("tui", a slang word in Cantonese) which means that the lecturer is lazy, unenthusiastic and that the course exams are made easy to pass. Paradoxically to what you may have heard from students that they opt for easy courses, they actually despise courses which they feel are "flat" and meaningless. They won't treat these courses seriously and degrade them into just "getting a few credits". (Chu Ming Chung – Physics)

Rather than making life easy for their students, the quotations in this section show that the excellent teachers were pleased to be seen as demanding. Lo Wai Luen was proud of her reputation for expecting a lot from students:

Generation after generation of students know that I'm tricky, fierce, fastidious and I make them work a lot. Right from the very first lesson, I will tell them very clearly my expectations and requirements. I will give them the course outlines and references. Also, I'll tell them that they can reselect modules after the first week and, if they prefer not to change, they should not regret ever choosing my subjects. They consciously know what to expect. (Lo Wai Luen – Chinese Literature)

Eleven of the 18 interviewees explicitly mentioned having demanding expectations of students. In addition, the three teachers from the medical faculty said their integrated curriculum was demanding on students.

There were contrasting ways of pushing students towards these high expectations. The quotations above and below show that there were occasions when some felt it was necessary to be fierce or angry. If high standards were not met they were prepared to show their displeasure.

Another element that might be worth mentioning is getting angry. I become fierce when students aren't taking it seriously. It happens once or twice a year. That's because I need to hold these people to high standards. If people haven't done the reading, I am a little more tolerant and I get somewhat angry. But if they aren't really thinking, I can become fierce. Is that good? I think it probably is, because I am not simply telling them to memorize things that aren't important; I'm telling them to think. If they refuse to think, they should not be in the university. (Gordon Mathews – Anthropology)

Another teacher tried to push students towards their achievement limits. To do this successfully it was necessary to know students as individuals and treat them individually.

You can be very tough. If they feel that they have learnt something, they appreciate it more. It's just like raising kids. You have to push your students to a limit. Some may like it, some may not. Different students may have different limits. You have to push them according to their own characters and personal limits. (Soung Liew – Information Engineering)

Good teachers have high expectations of students.

The occasional fierceness and anger mentioned in previous quotations was not universal. Other teachers felt they could achieve their expectations through a softer approach. Some had more subtle ways of getting students to meet their demands.

I think everyone has a different personality. By nature, I am not a tough teacher. I cannot behave like a tough teacher; it's just not me. I realized that some of my colleagues are quite tough and it works well for them. For example, when students use mobile phones in class, they will stop the class. I usually stop them by making some jokes or teasing the students. It seems to work. (Zhang Shuzhong – Operations Research)

An appropriate amount of work has to be set if learning is to occur. That work has to be done, though there can be some negotiation over deadlines if other assignments are due at the same time.

Another change is that I understand students' workload more. I put myself in their shoes. There are so many assignments and so many deadlines to meet. Every professor gives so much work. If appropriate, I will postpone the deadline for my work so that it won't clash with other deadlines. They may moan when you assign work, but deep down inside they know that it's for their own good. Students know which professors truly want to see them learn. (John Lui – Computer Science and Engineering)

Being Enthusiastic as a Teacher

The first way the teachers had for motivating students was through their own enthusiasm. One type of enthusiasm was for their discipline.

> But above all, it's somebody who can convey the enthusiasm that they themselves feel to make the subject matter interesting. (Gordon Mathews – Anthropology)

The next quotation combines enthusiasm for the subject with humanistic concerns:

> The teacher has to be enthusiastic about his subject. If he treats it mechanically, the students can feel it. If you can't feel excited about your subject, why should they? So enthusiasm is the basic requirement; enthusiasm to do their best and not to give up. We have to maintain our enthusiasm towards people as we are inclined to make other people's lives better by reducing sufferings. We hope to impart such attitudes to our students by setting up a good model within ourselves. (John Lui – Computer Science and Engineering)

There is also enthusiasm for teaching. Even towards the end of a long career, new courses and classes can still be something to be anticipated with excitement.

> In my life, teaching is something that I love most. It has to be colourful. If it were the same old thing all the time, it would have been impossible to be enjoyable. Every year, I long to have a new class. Even though I will be teaching the same course, I'll have a new approach and new discovery. I get excited every beginning of an academic year. I'm now 63. My students can see that I'm so animated in class because my life is there in my teaching and in enjoying seeing them learn. (Lo Wai Luen – Chinese Literature)

The teachers see motivating students as part of their role. They can also generate their own enthusiasm for teaching from their concern for their students. Taking a student-centred perspective not only leads to being a better teacher, but also leads to a more fulfilling relationship with the students, and this enhances the pleasure of teaching.

> I have always been very enthusiastic about teaching. I treat my students as younger brothers and sisters in mastery. They always remind me of my own growth and the mistakes I made. I'll try to teach them how to avoid the wrong paths and the mistakes. In the past, I was not methodical in my teaching and I was inclined to teach too much, so that students would be too full to digest and assimilate what I had taught. I have then learnt that I should be more student-oriented. I might have to somewhat readjust my expectation of students to a realistic level. (Francis Chan – Medicine and Therapeutics)

Some of the teachers were so enthusiastic about teaching that they taught courses for sixth form students on Saturdays.

Some of our teachers volunteer to teach little courses for sixth formers in secondary schools on Saturdays without any compensation because they want to enthuse young people about learning statistics. The department hasn't credited them the hours they devoted in this endeavour. They still do it because they are enthusiastic about teaching. (Fan Jianqing – Statistics)

Make it Enjoyable

Enthusiasm is more likely to be displayed if the classes are enjoyable. An enjoyable atmosphere can be brought about in two ways. Firstly, by the teacher adopting a light-hearted approach to the students:

> You don't have to stand in the front and lecture sternly and show off your knowledge to be a good teacher. A lot of this is pretty boring. Teaching can be enjoyable and still you learn from it. (Allan Walker – Educational Administration)

The other way is through finding interesting material and teaching it in a way which appeals to students' imagination. Doing this meant spending time working on developing materials and teaching approaches, and revising them in the light of feedback and observations.

> Therefore, other than being clear in our presentation, it is very important that we teachers project a positive image of our subject and set good behavioural examples for students. If you show that you are serious and excited about your subject, students will follow suit. This in turn will keep your enthusiasm alive and you'll be more happy teaching.

> I try to get into this exciting circle as soon as the semester begins. I convey to students that my course is very important and the course material is excellent. To achieve this, I myself shouldn't feel bored when preparing the teaching materials. I'll review and modify my teaching materials every two or three years. (Chu Ming Chung – Physics)

Through a Variety of Active Learning Approaches

The previous chapter described a variety of methods and approaches to teaching the teachers employed because of their suitability for helping the students achieve particular learning outcomes. There was an additional rationale for employing teaching methods which involved the students in active learning experiences, since they helped motivate the students. Changing the approach as the course progressed provided variety. As the students developed, they also responded better to more student-centred approaches.

> The use of teaching methods depends on the objectives of that course, students' characteristics, needs and prior knowledge at various stages. You should not use the same one method throughout the whole course. Teaching methods vary from

lesson to lesson. For the first lesson, I have to introduce myself and understand my students, their characters, needs and expectations. You cannot use the same approach in Lesson 21! Add and remove different elements as you go along so that your strategy fits in with the stage of development of your students. (Andrew Chan – Marketing)

The following quotation also shows that motivation can be enhanced by using a mixture of types of teaching methods. The same strategy all the time can become boring, particularly if it is a type which does not require active involvement.

In some classes, I use problem-based learning although I don't use that for the whole course. In my Masters course last year, I did it half in a traditional fashion, lecturing activities, and so forth, and the other half in problem-based learning. Before the problem-based learning, I'll give a lecture to get them to take that knowledge and skills; then their job is to apply it in the problem-based learning. I have never seen a student falling asleep in a problem-based learning classroom, whereas it does happen in a traditional classroom. The Masters students like the problem-based learning but they also like their lecture-type thing. That's one way of doing it. With my BEd students, I do a lot of cooperative learning. I will put them in a group from day one. I let them choose themselves. I help them work through and clarify the values and beliefs the group have as a way to get them together. (Allan Walker – Educational Administration)

Twelve of the interviewees said they used a variety of approaches to teaching, specifically as a motivational strategy. In the previous chapter, it was noted that all of the exemplary teachers had described at least one method of teaching, other than conventional lectures, seminars or tutorials. The rationale in that case was its suitability for achieving particular learning outcomes.

Through Relevant Content

In Chapter 3 one of the principles was to ensure that content included in a course could be perceived as relevant. The discussion of this principle in Chapter 3 focused mainly on the importance of relevance as an aspect of good curriculum design. An additional reason for ensuring that content is relevant is that it is a source of motivation. Students are much keener to learn about a topic if they can see that it will have practical relevance in the local situation.

I try to make the teaching materials as relevant as possible to local situation. I use a lot of examples. For example, I refer to local cases such as Hong Kong mortgages. How do you compute interest statements? Students feel that these questions are real and practical. (Zhang Shuzhong – Operations Research)

Searching for relevant materials can be a major part of the curriculum development process. With the amount of material produced for news and entertainment nowadays there is a lot to search through. That also means, though, that most topics have something of relevance which students can relate to.

> I try to make my lectures interesting and I bring in lots of examples and I try to use funny stories whenever I can. I use cartoons from the newspapers, still work drawings, anything that keeps the course lively.

> For example, a group decision-making exercise which is very well known. Recently, there was a good movie called "Thirteen Days" which dealt with the United States–Cuban missile crisis back in 1962. This movie has a sustained 20 to 25-minute segment in it that actually deals with the group decision-making process at the highest level of the U.S. government in 1962. It is very interesting. Hollywood occasionally supplies us with all these beautifully designed films that are historically accurate. By and large, that movie comes right out of some of the transcripts that existed of the day. It is an effective combination of things. (David Ahlstrom – Management)

All of the teachers referred to the importance of relevance in what was taught if students were to be interested and motivated by their teaching. Interest can be generated through readily available material if the teacher has enough imagination to see how it can relate to a topic.

> Sometimes, to further increase their interest, we'll watch a TV soap opera together. Last year, there was a series called "Love affairs in the office". We would watch the programme the night before and then discuss it the next day in the lecture. Some students commented that it was a good approach to many nice practical life examples. (Gordon Cheung – Management)

Inspiring and Encouraging Students

Relevance does not necessarily have to come from the teacher finding relevant material. It can also come from setting the students assignments which have some practical applications. The quotation below shows an example of this which the students evidently appreciated.

The quotation also illustrates another aspect of motivating students, namely the importance of giving praise for high achievement. At the start of the chapter the high demands of the excellent teachers were expounded. To motivate students it is important to encourage students by very explicitly applauding students when they meet the high expectations.

> Normally, final year students are required to write some software and make a presentation and I'll grade them on that. Some final year projects for the past few years have been excellent and we can actually use the software for students in the future. There is one piece of software about watching TV in the lab which was completed a couple of years back. I remember that year, there was a very popular TV programme on every evening. And the students who were still working in the lab would ask to watch the programme while they were there. The software is still

popular and running till now. I told my students: "You guys have reached a milestone. You have set certain standard about what a final year project should be. You are good models for future final year students to learn from. You've made a mark."

This is how I motivate my students: encourage them. If your boss or the VC comes and tells you, "Good job! Good job!" I'm sure you'll do more. In contrast, if they say, "You are not good enough … " you'll be demoralized. (John Lui – Computer Science and Engineering)

Conclusion

The excellent teachers all accepted that it was their responsibility to motivate students. They were demanding of their students, but accepted that their expectations would not be met unless they took positive steps to interest and motivate their students. The main steps adopted are summarized in the principle box below:

> Strategies for motivating students include:
> - the teacher displaying enthusiasm,
> - employing a variety of active learning approaches,
> - making classes enjoyable,
> - using relevant and interesting material, and
> - praising students when high expectations are met.

Chapter 7

Development as a Teacher

There are those who claim that good teachers are born not made. The excellent teachers interviewed in this study did not believe this. Many were prepared to admit that their teaching had not always been of the same high standard. This chapter is about how they had developed their teaching to its present exemplary standard.

> When I first started teaching, I did my best to stuff students with as much content as possible. I realize that this is not the right thing to do. On the contrary, I don't need to teach so much, and I should pace my teaching so that students can truly absorb what is being taught. There is knowledge of the world that can never all be taught. (John Lui – Computer Science and Engineering)

It is quite interesting that as many as half of the interviewees admitted that their teaching had improved considerably over the years. What is even more striking is that all of these admissions were to a common early problem—to trying to cover too much content. They came to realize that teaching something does not mean that the students learn it. Reducing the amount taught can lead to an increase in how much is learnt. It is possible that the teachers developed their beliefs about teaching from a teacher-centred, content-oriented position to one which was more student-centred and learning-oriented (Kember, 1997).

> I have learnt that it is no use to introduce a new concept in the last five minutes. There is no need to rush. I might not be able to cover the materials that I have prepared for the class due to class variations or students asking questions. In the early years of my teaching, I rushed through to cover everything planned. Now I teach them to understand rather than to rush through with the materials. I will have to repeat them again at the beginning of the next lesson anyway. (Fan Jianqing – Statistics)

Modelling on Past Teachers

One very common influence on the approach to teaching is the role modelling through being taught. All university teachers have spent many hours as the students of a host of teachers at school and at university. It is inevitable that these experiences impact upon their own teaching.

> I wasn't good at teaching at the beginning. I realized that responses from my students weren't good enough. I then tried to think of ways to improve and adopt new teaching methods. Sometimes, I will observe how good teachers teach. I have had an experience of getting ideas from observing how someone is teaching car mechanics. He taught so badly I knew what to avoid! He just talked to himself

and never looked at the students. He would continue talking without realizing that his students were having difficulties catching up. Trying to learn from good teachers is a good way. Avoid ineffective teaching techniques as demonstrated in poor teaching. You need to assimilate good teaching into your own practice as you are the one who knows your class best, so appropriate modification is necessary. Be committed to make improvements. (Andrew Chan – Marketing)

It is possible to learn from both good and poor teachers. Poor teachers show what not to do. Good teachers act as role models.

I have learnt from the few good teachers that I came across when I was a student. They explored complex knowledge in depth and explained it to us in simple ways. They showed us how to use basic core knowledge to logically and systematically solve problems. Poor teachers would speak incessantly showing you slide after slide, giving you notes that were ten inches thick, but in the end the main themes were blurred. The good ones demonstrated the main themes within the first ten minutes of their lessons, and you would know that this is the way to approach problems. Their presentation was so clear that I can still vividly remember the stuff being taught, and can apply what I was taught 30 years ago to solve problems today. (Gregory Cheng – Medicine and Therapeutics)

Through Colleagues

Another influence upon teaching was from colleagues. As teaching is a major component of academic work, it is a natural topic of conversation when colleagues meet over lunch or coffee.

We exchange ideas. We talk a lot over lunch. (Zhang Shuzhong – Operations Research)

Conversations like this are informal, but can be just as effective as more formal meetings. When colleagues talk about teaching it is more likely that courses will be coordinated.

Not in a systematic way. Informally, for example over lunch, we do learn from each other and exchange ideas about the methods, the textbooks they use, the best way to communicate with students. We also complain about students among ourselves. (Soung Liew – Information Engineering)

Food or drink seemed to be a necessary prerequisite for getting together to talk about teaching. If it was not over lunch, coffee was necessary:

Every morning I'll prepare coffee. You can see my coffee maker here! My colleagues who belong to the same team for the Astronomy course in GE will come along. We share our ideas over cups of coffee. This morning, a colleague was saying how useful a video was for demonstrating the telescope and how animated the students were. So we know students' responses to various teaching aids and methods. This is important since students differ in interest each year.

Through informal chit-chat we actually learn from each other. (Chu Ming Chung – Physics)

Attending Workshops

A further developmental influence mentioned by some of the interviewees was workshops about teaching:

> Participation in teaching workshops reinforces my ideas for improvement. For instance, I used to speak very fast but now I am conscious to slow down for students. My presentation becomes more focused as I leave out more unnecessary details. I can see my shortcomings and find ways to overcome them. (Leung Sing Fai – Clinical Oncology)

Soung Liew was quoted at length in Chapter 5, giving a description of how he used problem-based teaching. He said that the idea for doing this had come from a workshop:

> About four years ago, I attended a three- to four-hour course organized by the Teaching Development Unit. The course was about how to encourage interaction with students. They called it the problem-solving approach. I was influenced by this course. After taking the course, I decided to include problem-solving approach discussion sessions in my course. I give them open-ended problems. They are supposed to discuss the problems among themselves with assistance from lecturers and TAs. (Soung Liew – Information Engineering)

Good teaching can be developed through:
- learning from past teachers,
- exchanging ideas with colleagues, and
- attending workshops.

Feedback for Evaluation

Chapter 3 introduced a four-element model for curriculum development, of which one of the elements was feedback for evaluation. Feedback is used by the excellent teachers to improve both course design and individual teaching. As these teachers recognized the need to develop a relationship with their students, the students felt comfortable providing feedback. Feedback which was supplied was taken note of.

Constantly, your students are offering suggestions to improve your teaching. To resist appropriate changes is an attitudinal problem. If you are open-minded, you can make relevant improvements. Not all suggestions are reasonable. In some cases, you can modify and improve what students suggest. (Andrew Chan – Management)

The following quotation illustrates the use of feedback for refining an individual's teaching and improving curriculum design. Feedback was gathered through informal discussion with students and through evaluation questionnaires.

I gather feedback from students asking questions, at the end of the class, as they are unwilling to ask questions during lectures. Evaluation forms are very useful, particularly the part where students can write and express their frustrations; for example, the project is too difficult, and so forth. These are much more useful than number punching. It gives you good general guidelines.

The Department pays attention to teaching. In our discussion, we talk a lot about how to improve the way we teach: forming smaller classes, getting feedback from student representatives on our courses. They do give important feedback based on which we restructure our courses to meet their needs. (Soung Liew – Information Engineering)

In each of the quotations in this section the interviewees indicated that they did not rely solely on the standard course evaluation questionnaire for feedback. In the above two quotations and the one below, the additional source of feedback for evaluation is direct conversation with students. For this to be used to gather feedback on teaching is an indication of the level of rapport between the teacher and students.

Students also indicate to me that I am getting better. I ask for students' feedback openly and directly. Those so called objective evaluations, such as course evaluation questions, may not provide details specific enough for individual teachers as there may be sensitive issues involved and students tend not to write them down in a formal, predetermined questionnaire. We would rather ask for feedback directly from students. (Leung Sing Fai – Clinical Oncology)

The standard course evaluation questionnaire in use at the time did not give sufficient diagnostic information for improving teaching, and so several of the excellent teachers supplemented it with questionnaires of their own design. The ideas and questions included in the quotation below are useful in that they indicate how improvements can be made:

I designed my own course evaluation sheet. The main concern is whether students have enough examples. Am I am going too fast in presenting course materials? Do I give enough exercises and homework, and if I give enough assistance in that respect? They really suggest I slow down and repeat and speak loudly. They requested me to put notes earlier on the internet so that they would have the notes before they come to my class. But I told them that I prefer to reorganize my lecture notes after the class so that they are more of use to students after knowing what they may find difficult and need more explanation. So my own course evaluation help me find out the small things that I was not aware of, which turn out to be important in terms of helping students understand my class. (Zhang Shuzhong – Operations Research)

Another questionnaire used by one of the teachers also had open questions. It is more likely that students will respond to these open-ended questions on a teacher's questionnaire, than to those on the standard questionnaire, as the students know that the teacher wants their feedback and will act upon it.

From time to time, I give questionnaires to students asking them to write three aspects that they like about my class and three they don't like. They can write as many as they like. These questionnaires reveal that students find the overviews in the second session most helpful because they have been given a detailed lecture in the first session. Then we can step out, strip the details and just emphasize the important. (Fan Jianqing – Statistics)

Self-Reflection

Feedback is only useful if the teacher reflects upon it and makes use of the information to improve teaching and the curriculum. Continual reflection and refinement of teaching are one of the hallmarks of an excellent teacher.

My teaching is improving continuously. I reflect upon my practice as I go along. Personally, I constantly reflect upon my teaching and seek to improve my skills almost daily. I think of ways to enhance students' learning so that they can retain the knowledge and skills for a long time and apply them appropriately. It will be great if I can make the learning process enjoyable. (Leung Sing Fai – Clinical Oncology)

John Chi Kin Lee observes that the mechanism of reflection and action learning should be an integral facet of teaching in universities and schools. In the action learning cycle the teacher reflects upon feedback, which leads to action taken in an effort to improve teaching. If observation and feedback gathering continue, the process becomes an ongoing cycle of refining teaching and student learning.

Learning is an internalization experience. I think action learning is important in the context of education. Reflection is also important. In psychological terms, it means meditation. You should have reflection on what you have learnt. Application of action learning is important. For example, a student should be able to practise action learning in his/her teaching. Students who have no real teaching experience can apply action learning while they are practising their mock teaching lessons in schools. Students should also observe and study the actual teaching practices and use this information to support their own reflections. (John Chi Kin Lee – Curriculum and Instruction)

> To improve teaching it is necessary to gather feedback, reflect upon it and then act on the reflections.

Handling the Tension Between Teaching and Research

In a university there is inevitably tension between the two main roles of an academic—namely, teaching and research. The interviews showed evidence of two ways of dealing with this tension: firstly by accepting the importance of teaching, and secondly by establishing a relationship between teaching and research.

Importance of Teaching

All of the excellent teachers recognized the importance of teaching. They also felt that research was important. Winning an exemplary teaching award does not come at the expense of research.

> Teaching and research are both important. In weighing the two, I prefer to spend more time in teaching. To publish one paper more, or one paper less, is to do with personal attainment. However, if I don't teach well, the damage is far reaching. Our faculty's mission is an equal emphasis on teaching and research. Sometimes, it's difficult to manage both equally well. If I pay more attention to teaching, that more or less will delay my research. (Chan Hung Kan – Chinese Language)

Research and teaching were seen as integral components of being an academic. Everybody has to do both—and do them well!

> I see research and teaching as a whole package and it's not something that is separable. Just like you can't take the job, the salary and the vacations, but not the responsibility. (John Lui – Computer Science and Engineering)

Relationship Between Teaching and Research

The other way of handling teaching and research was by finding ways in which they could complement each other. Rather than the two being in competition for time, they could be mutually beneficial.

The benefits could flow in either direction. In the first example the teaching receives the benefit from the research. The research provides a relevant current application of a technique. A topic which might have been taught as abstract theory comes alive because of knowledge of its application through research. We were certainly interested to know that the tape recorder used to record the interviews relied on regression!

Everybody is different; many of our colleagues are good teachers and they are always ranked very highly by students. They are competent and articulate and they have a language advantage. [Most of them are Cantonese speakers while Professor Fan is a Putonghua speaker.] If I am different, it is probably due to my research interest and my connection with many people in the real world. I can instantly illustrate the application of certain techniques to students with up-to-date real life examples. For instance, the data compression technique in your digital recorder here is illustrating regression technique. An engineer can then apply and carry it over, actually programme it and make the data compressed. As to that part, it is beyond our class. But the first part, the "how" and the "why" is within statistics. I know the technique and the application through my research and I can use it as an example to teach my students. In this way, my own research also benefits my teaching. (Fan Jianqing – Statistics)

For the other two quotations in this section, the flow is in the opposite direction; research ideas emanating from teaching. It is perhaps less common to visualize research benefiting from teaching, but the interviews provided examples.

However, the two are not mutually exclusive either. Some of my research papers are inspired by my teaching. During my teaching preparation, I will discover areas in which I want to know more. For instance, while teaching the infusion of spoken Cantonese into written text, I realize that we need some kind of benchmarking. In Hong Kong, nobody has raised this issue before. So I can publish something in this area to raise awareness.

There are a couple of papers published concerning Cantonese language which are the result of my teaching. One summer, some students and I went around and interviewed a few secondary schools with approximately 200 students to investigate their phonetic problems. The result got published in an educational journal. This all started from teaching phonetics. This is to demonstrate that research and teaching are not two conflicting entities. (Chan Hung Kan – Chinese Language)

These examples of how teaching can benefit research, and vice versa, are of interest in the light of the many studies which compare research and teaching quality. Most of these look for correlations between teacher evaluation ratings and the number of publications. A meta-analysis of this body of research (Hattie & Marsh, 1996) found that the correlation between the two was effectively zero. In a further study, Marsh and Hattie (2002) examined alternative models of possible relationships, but found further evidence of no correlation. They concluded that research productivity and teaching effectiveness, as measured by student ratings, are independent constructs. Possibly the concentration on readily available measures has meant that more qualitative synergies between other aspects of teaching and research have been missed.

I am conducting research in universalism at the moment. This all began from designing a course on the same topic for General Education. As I had not taught this subject before, I had to do a lot of research into it so as to be well equipped for my teaching. During the process of course preparation, I discovered great research interest in the topic. (Chu Ming Chung – Physics)

The tension between teaching and research can be handled by recognizing the importance of teaching, and seeking synergies between teaching and research.

Chapter 8

Is Quality in Teaching Culturally Specific?

Up to this point the major part of the book has concentrated on deriving principles of good teaching from the interviews with the excellent teachers. Now that the reporting of this analysis is complete, it is appropriate to examine the set of principles which have been derived against relevant literature. Direct contrast is not straightforward since it is hard to find other studies which precisely match this one. Comparison with models of good teaching is also difficult as Chapter 1 has shown that these are quite diverse, reflecting a variety of theoretical or atheoretical origins.

The questions which are likely to be of most interest to readers are related to applicability. Could these same principles be used in other universities as a guiding framework for quality in teaching? Alternatively, are they in some way culturally specific? If so, what are the boundaries of the cultural identity?

This chapter makes a series of comparisons of the previous analysis with other studies which either investigated exemplary teachers or considered teaching from a Hong Kong or Chinese cultural perspective. It is, therefore, necessary to compare the principles of good teaching with the following areas of literature:

- other studies of teachers given awards for exemplary teaching in Western universities,
- research into teachers and teaching in schools in Hong Kong and China, and
- research into university teachers' beliefs about teaching. This will concentrate upon research in Hong Kong, but will also need to make comparisons with similar work in the West.

Exemplary Teachers

It is surprising how few other studies there are of award-winning university teachers. Dunkin and Precians (1992) interviewed 12 award-winning teachers and compared their comments with those of novice teachers. The results are discussed further in Dunkin (2002). The study identified four main dimensions to effective teaching: as structuring learning, as motivating learning, as encouraging activity and independence, and as establishing interpersonal relationships. Experts showed a greater frequency in mentioning these dimensions than novices. The semiquantitative method of analysing the data meant that a more detailed characterization of good teaching was not produced.

Ballantyne, Bain, and Packer (1997) conducted interviews with 44 exemplary teachers from a wide range of universities in Australia. The outcomes of the project were reported as individual stories from each of the teachers. Without detailed analysis across the interviews there was no resulting set of common principles or dimensions of good teaching to compare with those from this study.

School Teachers in Hong Kong

There has been sufficient research into teachers and teaching in Hong Kong and China to justify an edited book titled *Teaching the Chinese learner: Psychological and pedagogical perspectives* (Watkins & Biggs, 2001). The back cover claims that the book:

> … analyses the ways in which teachers in Hong Kong and China think about their teaching, and the ways in which they conduct their teaching. Differences between Chinese and Western approaches to teaching are identified, and lessons drawn for educational reform.

An earlier book on the "Chinese learner" (Watkins & Biggs, 1996) had focused on what has become known as the paradox of the Chinese learner. Commentators believed they observed Chinese learners using approaches to learning which led to poor outcomes in the West, yet Chinese students performed very well in comparisons with international counterparts. The book on teaching (Watkins & Biggs, 2001) also presents a paradox, this time in two parts. One part of the paradox concerns the strict, stern or authoritarian approach adopted by Chinese parents and teachers following Confucian tradition (D. Y. F. Ho, 1986, 1996; Salili, 1996). This is discussed in the section on "Authoritarian teachers".

Teaching and Learning in Schools

The other part of the paradox applies to the method of teaching and the learning outcomes. Watkins and Biggs (2001) state it as:

> Given that teachers in Confucian-heritage cultures operate under substandard classroom conditions in terms of Western standards, and that CHC students perform so well, how do these teachers do it? How can teachers engage students in productive learning activities when they teach large numbers at a time, in an expository manner, in which the students' role is essentially passive? Do students learn in spite of, or because of, the way teachers operate in their classrooms? (p. 3)

The paradox of the Chinese learner applied equally to school and university students. It is debatable though to what extent the teaching paradoxes are applicable to universities. It is noteworthy that the section in the book on "teacher practice", which contains the work relevant to the paradoxes, has six chapters drawing on research in schools and just one on universities. This university-based chapter (Stokes, 2001) does not touch on the paradoxes as it examines staff perceptions of the introduction of problem-based learning into one university programme.

The paradox in the quotation above arises as a result of conditions in the Hong Kong school system. The class sizes are large, with classes of around 40 being quite typical. The manner of teaching is dictated by the Hong Kong Examinations Authority, which is an autonomous body in charge of all public examinations (Watkins & Biggs, 2001). Success in examinations is vital as it determines entry to the final two years of secondary school and then to university. Hong Kong still has an elitist education system with only about one third of the age group able to gain entry to Secondary 6 (Education and Manpower Bureau, 2003). The numbers in the education system are then nearly halved again by entry to the first year of entry to UGC universities (University Grants Committee of Hong Kong, 2003). In a culture where education is highly valued this places enormous pressure on teachers to coach students to pass the examinations. The pressure goes right back down the educational chain to the kindergartens, which prepare children for entry to the more elite schools with a better record in getting students through the examinations (Education Commission, 1999).

A number of the interviews contain comments about the effects of the school system on students who enter university.

> Unfortunately, in Hong Kong education, they are not trained to discuss and debate at primary and secondary levels. It's difficult for them to put down the old mode of learning and pick up discovery. … Students who grow up in Hong Kong, however, are generally frightened as they are so used to having model answers given to them in their secondary school training. "You just give me the model answers, tell me all about the author and I will memorize, so that I can regurgitate during exams". There were times when students were really frightened and dissatisfied with the fact that I had not given them the absolute model answers. So, it takes rather a long time to convince the students that the teacher is not there to tell me everything or hand down knowledge. It is I myself who need to think independently, analyse, discover and eventually understand. (Lo Wai Luen – Chinese Literature)

The factors leading to this type of education in schools have little relevance to teaching in universities. Staff–student ratios in universities in Hong Kong are comparable to those in the West. They may well be higher, as budget cuts have only recently had a major impact upon Hong Kong universities, whereas those in many Western countries have suffered financial stringencies for decades. Universities are autonomous in their assessment practices. They are, therefore, at liberty to design assessment which is conducive to the types of enlightened teaching practices documented in this book.

Authoritarian Teachers

The applicability of the stern or authoritarian paradox was investigated by searching the transcripts for these and related terms. Only two teachers used the term "stern". One said she had moved away from this approach. The other was a teacher educator who discussed the concept in terms of training future school teachers.

The stance of the excellent teachers towards their students was discussed in Chapter 6. The conclusion reached there was that they were demanding, because of their high expectations. This did not, though, imply that they were authoritarian. To the contrary several reported taking quite a soft line and all managed to establish a very good rapport with their students.

Zhang Shuzhong recalled his own schooling being influenced by an authoritarian regime (no pain, no gain). However, later education in the West changed his view of teaching.

> I grew up in Shanghai where teachers are very demanding and they believe in "no pain, no gain". It's part of the educational process that you cannot avoid in Chinese culture. I spent eleven years in Holland where my concept of teaching was formed. There I found out that learning doesn't have to be painful. The effort you pay is not proportional to the amount of pain, whereas in China, we believe that this is the case. I realize that I can work for hours and not feeling the pain because people, by nature, are curious. (Zhang Shuzhong – Operations Research)

I. T. Ho (2001) accepted that there was some evidence of Chinese school teachers being more authoritarian in class than their Western counterparts. She also found, however, that Chinese teachers tended to differ more in their in- and out-of-class behaviour. The formality of the classroom could differ from a more friendly behaviour towards students out of class (I. T. Ho, 1999).

While there is little evidence of the authoritarian behaviour of Chinese school teachers influencing the in-class approach of university teachers, there is some evidence of the CUHK teachers adopting a very friendly pose towards their students out of class. Examples of these friendship-building activities were given in Chapter 5.

> It's my obligations. Many people joke on me that I have sold myself to the University. I spend lots of time with students. Anytime they come, I spend time to talk with them. Students come to me not only for academic matters but also for sharing of opinions and something personal. ... As a result, I have to spend lots of time with my students. I leave the office late, work on Saturdays and Sundays, am late to bed. (Kenneth Leung – Journalism)

There is insufficient evidence to determine how widespread the practice of developing rapport with students through out-of-class contact is. It is possible that the levels of out-of-class socialization are somewhat higher than that for Western university teachers, but not by a great extent.

Applicability of Research into School Teachers

There appears to be reasonable evidence of Hong Kong and Chinese school teachers following practices and holding beliefs which show some distinction from those elsewhere. There appears to be little sign of these practices having any applicability or influence on university teachers in Hong Kong, except possibly for out-of-class contact.

While students entering universities in Hong Kong have been clearly influenced by the school system they have been immersed in for many years, the strategies used in university teaching in Hong Kong do not appear to be significantly affected by the nature of the school system. School and university teaching seem to be distinct professions, and the cultural influence found in school teaching is not noticeable in universities. The next section discusses possible reasons for this.

Cultural Boundaries of Teaching Practice

Stigler and Hiebert (1999) compared school teaching in Germany, Japan and the United States by videotaping classrooms in the three countries. The conclusion which was relevant to this work is that they "were amazed at how much teaching varied across cultures and how little it varied within cultures" (p. 11). This finding may appear to be at odds with the conclusion reached in the previous section, unless it is remembered that this was a school-based study.

The insights into good teaching derived from interviews with teachers at a university in Hong Kong which are described in this book have a limited relationship to conclusions drawn from studies of Hong Kong school teachers. However, models of excellent practice derived from a Hong Kong university would appear to resemble, in many respects, enlightened ideals in the Western university system.

While it might, at first, appear that the conclusions of this study contradict the quoted conclusion of Stigler and Hiebert, they can be interpreted as being highly consistent with it if the cultural boundaries are carefully defined. There appears to be little cultural influence between school and university teachers. The practices and ideals of school and university teachers in Hong Kong are sufficiently different to conclude that they are not part of a common culture.

Instead, there would appear to be a logic in ascribing university teachers to an international culture, which applies to those in universities of a reputable international standard. This conclusion is justifiable on grounds beyond the findings of this study.

As universities have been founded it has been common practice for them to try to strengthen their reputation by striving to follow as far as possible the configuration of universities held in the highest regard. In this respect Oxbridge and the Ivy League universities have served as a model for practice, even if the ideal has not always been reached.

Procedures for maintaining standards across university systems serve to reinforce the cultural uniformity of striving for a common model. For example, the external examiner system, which has been widely adopted in the British Commonwealth, was introduced with the rationale of achieving uniformity of degree standards across universities. Such a quality assurance system can only operate if there is a degree of homogeneity in the practices of universities.

The influence of overseas university systems is strengthened through academics receiving education overseas. Of the 15 Chinese excellent teachers, 12 took at least one of their degrees in overseas universities. This time in overseas universities is particularly important in the light of the comments quoted in Chapter 7, which showed that former teachers had one of the strongest influences on development as a teacher.

> I did my PhD abroad. ... I remember when I was in Graduate School (UCLA), there was a course that started at 8 in the morning. For a lot of students, it's hard to get up and attend a lecture at 8 a.m. But every time I came out of his lecture, I felt packed with energy and ready for the day. He taught something very abstract. In the last lesson, when he announced that the course was over, all the students gave him a standing ovation. (John Lui – Computer Science and Engineering)

A further influence towards globalization comes from the practices of the academic tribes which make up a discipline (Becher, 1989). Members of the tribe work towards the common icon of publications in the more prestigious journals. International networks form through contacts at conferences, and are then reinforced in this era of information technology.

It is, therefore, perfectly credible that the excellent teachers in this study would see themselves as having a common culture with colleagues in other universities of a reputable standard, and particularly so with those in their discipline. However, affinity to a discipline does not seem to have resulted in disciplinary distinctions between visions of quality in teaching, as the principles derived from the interviews were consistent across disciplines.

University professors and school teachers have always been regarded as quite distinct professions. School teachers tend to have a national rather than an international outlook, so it is not surprising that there are distinct cultures between school teaching in different countries. It is also reasonable to assume that these cultures have limited impact on university teachers in a particular country, who are themselves part of a quite distinct international university culture. Kenneth Leung's observations show that he is convinced that teaching at school is quite different to that at university.

> I always challenge my students that university education should not be the same as secondary education. Students should not only know how to answer questions, but also how to ask questions. You can ask only if you know where the problem is. Can you identify problems from the superficial facts or phenomena? Lots of teachers can't help students in that sense until they are trained. Therefore, I think my subject helps students challenge the cases given to them.

> One of the main purposes of my teaching is enhancing those undergraduate students' understanding of university education. It is not something they can comfortably sit with. They should rigorously challenge their own conventional thinking—the way they think, the way they look at observable phenomenon so as to be able to learn how to learn. That's the crux of learning how to learn, the ability to identify the problem. If you are able to ask questions, you will find the answers.

> They are learning not only to get credits but also how to face the data, observable phenomenon and decision-making. That's why the most frequent comment in both undergraduate and graduate students' course evaluation is "highly inspirational". It is exciting. I think it is from students who don't have sufficient preparation for this kind of training. (Kenneth Leung – Journalism)

University Teachers' Beliefs About Teaching

The literature on university teachers' beliefs about teaching needs to be examined because a paper by Pratt, Kelly, and Wong (1999) claimed to have identified a distinct Chinese conception of effective university teaching. The essence of this conception is captured by the following quotation:

> The primary responsibility of a teacher was to take students systematically through a clear set of tasks, high in structure and directed towards examination. As the first step, students are expected to copy, drill and memorize the basics, or "foundational" knowledge of their discipline in forms that closely resemble its presentation by the teacher and/or the text. The process of memorization was understood to be both purposeful and appropriate. (p. 248)

This conception is clearly completely at odds with the principles derived from the interviews with the teachers in this study. Principle 6, which calls for the development of self-managed learning ability through student-centred approaches to teaching, is not compatible with this conception. The exposure to conflicting theories suggested by Principle 7 is radically different from this conception.

Each of the principles derived in Chapter 4, on how teaching is performed are inconsistent with the purported conception. These principles call for a variety of teaching methods which involve teachers and students interacting together to discuss key concepts. The approach to teaching demands teaching methods and assessment being consistent with learning outcomes which are very different to memorizing basic knowledge.

The results are also inconsistent with the outcomes of a review of 13 studies of university teachers' beliefs about teaching (Kember, 1997). Ten of the 13 studies examined in the review gathered data through interviews with academics at universities in Australia and the United Kingdom. Two (Gow & Kember, 1993; Kember & Gow, 1994) collected data from universities in Hong Kong. The sample for the remaining study (Pratt, 1992) was from Canada, China, Hong Kong, Singapore and the United States. The review did not find differences between categories of beliefs about teaching conceptions between the studies in Western universities and those in Asia.

To the contrary, it was possible to produce a synthesized multiple-level model which subsumed all the reviewed research on beliefs about teaching in the 13 studies (Kember, 1997). The model contained five categories of beliefs subsumed under two broad orientations; one labelled teacher-centred/content-oriented, and the other student-centred/learning-oriented. These orientations and categories were shown to be reasonably consistent with all 13 studies, suggesting international applicability.

The conception of teaching assigned by Pratt et al. (1999) to Hong Kong academics lie towards the teacher-centred pole of the former orientation. The Western teachers in the sample were assigned to the student-centred orientation. Examination of the principles derived in the present study shows that the beliefs of the excellent teachers would clearly lie in the student-centred/learning-oriented orientation. The practices and espoused values of all the interviewees were incompatible with the other orientation.

The incompatibility of the claims of Pratt et al. (1999) with the results of this study and the substantial body of research into beliefs about teaching, can be explained by considering the sampling and analytical methods used by Pratt et al. (1999), though these are not explained as clearly as they might be. Their data were mostly gathered through a survey with open-ended questions. Responses were received from 397 students and 82 academic staff, with a response rate of just 14% from the latter. The breakdown of academic staff into the Chinese and Western samples is not reported, but Westerners are a small minority in universities in Hong Kong. Whatever the split, the Chinese sample would have been dominated by students and these would have been compared to a handful of Western academics.

The disparity in sampling was then compounded by the analytical procedure adopted which is reported as: "our findings are presented as differences between extremes" (p. 245). Chinese conceptions of teaching, therefore, effectively come from students, whereas Western conceptions of teaching come from a limited number of professors teaching in universities in Hong Kong. The conceptions of teaching of the Chinese sample, who are predominantly Chinese students, are then attributed to all Chinese teachers and students.

Kember (2001) analysed a set of interviews with 53 Hong Kong students. The interviewees were found to have consistent sets of beliefs about knowledge and the process of teaching and learning. Less experienced students tended to have beliefs in an orientation labelled didactic/reproductive. More experienced students in postgraduate courses reported having made the transition to a facilitative/transformative orientation. Kember, Jenkins, and Ng (2003) found that Hong Kong students' perceptions of good teaching were a function of their conceptions of learning. The majority of those interviewed had reproductive conceptions of learning, and so preferred didactic teaching. Students who had developed a self-determining conception of learning found facilitative teaching more helpful. It is, therefore, not surprising that a sample dominated by students, particularly if many came from initial years, could hold predominant beliefs of the type attributed by Pratt et al. (1999) to being the culturally dominant belief within universities in Hong Kong. This research into the beliefs about teaching and learning of Hong Kong students is consistent with observations expressed in the interviews.

> At university level, being able to understand well and yet be good at exams are two separate things. There are students who are excellent in exams in secondary level but only average in faculty exams. Their clinical performance and communication can be rather poor. This is due to the different requirements at university level. At secondary level, they are required to memorize a lot and to regurgitate during exams. At university level, it is not simply how much you memorize but, rather, how much you understand and how effectively you can convey your understanding. In the Faculty of Medicine, students have to face such tremendous amount of stuff to learn that they may not be able to prioritize their learning according to the degree of importance. Their problem with examinations is even greater. Our exams stress the ability to communicate. When they have a deficit in these skills and techniques in communicating, these are very hard for them to acquire.

> In our first meeting with students, I will tell them: You should throw away your accustomed ways of learning at secondary schools; otherwise, you will be banging your head against a great wall, and wondering why I was always top of the class in secondary schools and, now, I'm struggling to get by! (Francis Chan – Medicine and Therapeutics)

A more reasonable interpretation of the data for both Pratt et al. (1999) and this study is that both of the teaching belief orientations found in Kember's (1997) review exist in Hong Kong as they do in universities elsewhere. The teachers interviewed for this study subscribed to the student-centred/learning-oriented orientation, because the sample was of teachers awarded the Vice-Chancellor's award for exemplary teaching. The teacher-centred/content-oriented belief predominated in the study of Pratt et al. (1999) because their Hong Kong sample was mostly students.

Beliefs and Practices of Teachers

A model which explains well the strands of evidence discussed in this Chapter is that linking conceptions of teaching to approaches to practice as a teacher, to student approaches to learning, and in turn to student learning outcomes. This is a simplified version of one of the summative outcomes of Kember's (1997) review of research into academics' conceptions of teaching.

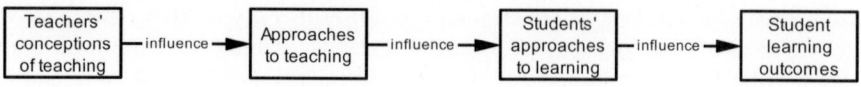

Figure 8.1. Links Between Teachers' Conceptions of Teaching and Student Learning Outcomes

There is good evidence for the links in the model. Two studies have characterized approaches to teaching in higher education (Kember & Kwan, 2000; Trigwell, Prosser, & Taylor, 1994) and both showed evidence that the approach adopted by teachers in the respective studies followed logically from those teachers' beliefs about teaching.

Gow and Kember (1993), and Kember and Gow (1994) showed, at the departmental level within universities, that teachers' beliefs about teaching influenced the approaches to learning students adopted in their courses. Trigwell, Prosser, and Waterhouse (1999) found comparable results with individual teachers. Sheppard and Gilbert (1991) produced case studies of teaching and learning in four departments. They found that the lecturer's theories of teaching impacted upon the development of students' epistemological development. Courses which considered alternative conceptions of knowledge were more likely to be associated with meaningful learning outcomes.

The teachers in this study clearly had beliefs in the orientation labelled student-centred/learning-oriented. These beliefs about teaching resulted in them adopting teaching practices or approaches consistent with these beliefs, which have been encapsulated as the set of principles of good teaching in this book. These practices in turn encouraged students to develop the high quality learning outcomes described in Chapter 4. The students recognized themselves as achieving these outcomes through the enlightened practice of these teachers, and so gave positive responses when the teaching was evaluated. This was a major factor in the teachers being nominated for awards in the first place.

There must also exist within the university a body of teachers with teacher-centred/content-oriented beliefs. If a set of these had been interviewed it is likely that there would also have been a high degree of commonality about their teaching practices, but these would have differed from the set of principles of good teaching derived from the excellent teachers.

These sets of beliefs and practices should be thought of as the poles of a spectrum rather than dichotomous categories. The exemplary teacher awards imply that the interviewees were regarded as the best teachers in the University. Inevitably there must also be a poorest set. Others are strung out between.

Kember and Kwan (2002) characterized approaches to teaching in terms of six continua, one for motivation and five for strategy. The majority of the interviewees were positioned near content-centred or learning-centred poles for most continua. Intermediate positions were not unusual though.

If university teachers in reputable universities are an international culture, each university will have its sets of teachers with the two belief orientations. Those with an orientation towards student-centred/learning-oriented beliefs are likely to define good teaching practice in a manner consistent with the principles of good teaching developed in this book. Those with the teacher-centred/content-oriented beliefs will adopt practices which are more didactic in nature.

If it is accepted that the excellent university teachers in this study are part of a global university culture, it implies that the derived principles of good teaching should be widely applicable. There is no reason why they should not be accepted as a model of good practice in university teaching in other reputable universities.

The set of principles can then be regarded as having some significance. The search for a commonly agreed definition of quality in teaching has been nearly as elusive as that for the Holy Grail. The set of principles of good teaching, derived by rigorous research techniques, from teachers judged to be excellent, have to be seen as a significant contribution to the important teaching quality agenda.

Chapter 9

Implications for Learning Enhancement

The starting point for this chapter draws upon the ending of the previous one. That showed a causal chain model in which teachers' conceptions of teaching influence their approaches to teaching, which in turn influence students' approaches to learning and learning outcomes. The implication of this model for enhancing the quality of teaching and learning is that the chances of fundamental improvement is likely to be influenced by the prevailing beliefs about teaching and learning of the teachers.

If teaching is not perceived as important, or if the predominant beliefs about teaching lie towards the transmissive pole, it is likely to be difficult to make significant changes to the quality of teaching and learning. Quality assurance measures or staff development issues which address teaching methods or approaches are unlikely to be effective if the aim is inconsistent with predominant teachers' beliefs.

Kember (1997) gave an example of one university requiring plans for new programmes to incorporate small group tutorials in their timetables. The university management had been convinced of the importance of active learning and interaction in teaching. They assumed that the tutorials would be used for discussion and active engagement of students in practical applications. This did happen in some cases, but observation of many of the classes revealed the teacher standing at the front giving a presentation or lecture. Teachers with a transmissive belief about teaching were not convinced of the need for discussion, and so taught the only way they knew how. Their courses consisted of lectures and minilectures.

Other examples of well-meaning top-down initiatives which have had limited impact can be found in the Hong Kong school sector. Perusal of the series of Education Commission reports reveals some very enlightened policy statements. However, topics like language of education, assessment and selection of students by schools keep recurring in successive reports. The processes of implementation through the top-down bureaucracy seem unable to bring about the changes in belief and practice necessary to put the policies into effect.

A good example was the Target Oriented Curriculum, which had the very laudable intention of reducing the relentless examination pressure on Hong Kong school students through the frequent, highly competitive, norm-referenced public examinations. The aim was to reduce the number of examinations and make the assessment more criterion-referenced. A number of commentators (Carless, 1998; Morris, 1998; Morris, Chan, & Lo, 1998; Biggs & Watkins,

2001) have pointed to the failure to implement the initiative in the form intended. A number of reasons have been given for this outcome, of which a highly significant one was the failure of the implementation strategies to address the beliefs, practices or needs of the front-line teachers. As long as they continued to see the vital importance of their students getting high examination grades, the practice of cramming and rehearsing for examinations prevailed.

Resistance to Changing Beliefs

These examples indicate the types of quality assurance initiative which often have little impact. However, the more important issue is that of determining the type of ventures which will positively affect the quality of teaching and learning. The discussion so far in this chapter has suggested that change for the better is more likely to occur if teachers' beliefs are taken into account. This leads to the next area of literature examined, which is on the persistence or deep-seated nature of fundamental beliefs.

Some of the most compelling evidence of the resistance of beliefs to change comes from research which shows how students can cling to erroneous or outdated conceptions of fundamental concepts despite being taught the accepted interpretation at some length. Dahlgren (1984) asked university economics students "Why does a bun cost about one (Swedish) crown?" The answers could be placed in one of two categories. The expected response would have referred to the concept of supply and demand, which is one of the most fundamental concepts taught in introductory economics courses. Despite passing their courses, though, a substantial proportion of the students gave an answer that the price equalled the value of the bun.

Similar examples are common in science, and particularly physics (Driver & Erickson, 1983; Helm & Novak, 1983; McDermott, 1984; Osborne & Wittrock, 1983; Pfundt & Duit, 1985; West & Pines, 1985). A common finding is students giving answers to simple everyday questions which indicate an Aristotelian conception of a phenomenon, such as a force, whereas the courses they had taken would have taught a Newtonian conception.

In the light of findings such as these the research in this area moved on to try to find ways to teach which would result in students changing conceptions of fundamental phenomena. From the field of science education, Champagne, Gunstone, and Klopfer (1985) reported how difficult the process of changing students' conceptions of physics phenomena is. They reported changes in conceptions after several day-long sessions of ideational conflict, and quotations from some of the students illustrate the demanding nature of the process.

These examples of resistance to conceptual change refer to students clinging on to ideas about phenomena included in their curriculum. For the case of teachers' beliefs about teaching, the conception is that of one of their two major roles in their professional lives. These beliefs would have formed over the span of their teaching careers. The findings in Chapter 7 that previous teachers were a fundamental developmental influence, suggest that our exemplary teachers' beliefs could also have been developing in their time as students. Beliefs about teaching would, thus, be fundamental to their view of academic life and have formed over a considerable period of time. This suggests that these beliefs might be more deep-seated and even harder to change than students' conceptions of phenomena.

Evidence of the persistence of teachers' beliefs about teaching comes from a review of teacher education programmes (Wideen, Mayer-Smith, & Moon, 1998). The review concluded that most programmes "have little effect upon the firmly held beliefs of the beginning teachers" (p. 130). Traditional courses which focused on the provision of propositional knowledge were found to be particularly ineffective because students filtered the knowledge through their existing belief set. Alternative programmes based on approaches such as reflective practice, action research or constructivist theory were more successful if they had an initial focus on the existing knowledge and beliefs of the beginning teachers.

Disciplinary Conventions

The international culture of university teaching, discussed in the previous chapter, affects the curriculum and the approach to teaching within disciplines, particularly in science, engineering and other professional disciplines. Professors within these disciplines see themselves as belonging to a disciplinary international tribe (Becher, 1989). At conferences, or tribal gatherings, an accepted wisdom develops about what should be included in a curriculum. This is then reinforced through the external examiner system and professional accreditation.

The core contents of disciplinary knowledge often pass from teacher to student. New academics base the content of their courses on what they themselves were taught. In some disciplines the core basic elements of the curriculum might have much in common between universities.

There is more diversity in courses dealing with the frontiers of knowledge. Degrees need to be seen to deal with recent developments; so cutting edge material must be included. As the pace of societal and technological change quickens, this means that more and more needs to be incorporated into curricula on top of the accepted fundamental disciplinary knowledge. As a result many curricula, particularly in technological subjects, have become very packed.

This may be an important contributing factor to student ratings of teaching in engineering and science tending to be on the low side (Barnes & Patterson,

1988; Cashin, 1995; Neumann & Neumann, 1985). This is an international trend and so is another indicator of the international disciplinary tribes.

Students find their courses overpacked which itself tends to depress ratings (Kember, 2004). The teachers stick to didactic teaching because they feel they need to cover the substantial body of content in the internationally accepted curriculum. Teaching which involves discussion and active student involvement is eschewed because it is perceived as leading to a reduction in content coverage. However, it is these more interactive forms of teaching, consistent with the principles derived in this book, which receive higher student ratings, because the students perceive them to be more effective forms of teaching and learning.

A fallacy in the drive to cover a substantial body of content through didactic teaching is that there is often a limited relationship between what is taught and what is learnt. Although material may be covered in lectures, it may not be understood or learnt in any meaningful way. There may be surface attempts to commit sufficient to memory to pass tests and examinations, but then all is forgotten.

Improving the quality of teaching and learning, therefore, often involves challenging both beliefs about teaching, and notions of what needs to be covered if a programme is to be consistent with disciplinary conventions, particularly in science and technology-related disciplines. There are, therefore, often two interrelated deep-seated beliefs to challenge if teachers are to improve the quality of their teaching.

This may sound like a daunting task, but at least one example of change at the level of the disciplinary tribe, rather than the individual teacher, exists. The accepted traditional view of the medical curriculum was that basic building blocks of foundation knowledge in the applied sciences needed to be covered first in the main body of the programme. Clinical practice did not appear until quite late. The focus on learning basic knowledge did little or nothing to develop the capabilities needed to practise as a doctor—such as diagnostic skills and the ability to communicate with patients. Over a number of years the medical tribe has undergone a disciplinary conversion to seeing problem-based learning as the accepted curriculum model. McMaster University is normally acknowledged as being the original evangelists (Neufeld & Barrows, 1974). The evidence that problem-based learning leads to better development of the types of capabilities needed by medical doctors (Kaufman & Mann, 1996; Newble & Clarke, 1987) has led to increasing numbers of medical faculties accepting the new tribal wisdom and changing to problem-based learning.

Conceptual Change Model

The pioneering work of Lewin (1952) on bringing about social change through group decision-making has been very influential on the topic of bringing about changes in the face of deep-seated beliefs. He suggested a three-step procedure: unfreezing, moving and then freezing at the new position.

Others have subsequently utilized this work in educational contexts. The three step process has remained, but with different emphasis. Strike and Posner (1985) characterized cognitive changes in students' understanding of science concepts in terms of advances, retreats and periods of indecision. Nussbaum and Novick (1982) and West (1988) suggested a similar three-phase process for bringing about conceptual change. These are:

- a process for diagnosing existing conceptual frameworks and revealing them to those involved;
- a period of disequilibrium and conceptual conflict which makes the subject dissatisfied with existing conceptions; and
- a reforming or reconstruction phase in which a new conceptual framework is formed.

A recent example from Hong Kong concerns changing postgraduate students' beliefs about teaching and learning away from those which Hong Kong students typically acquire from their schooling (see Chapters 4 and 8) towards beliefs which would enable them to construct their own knowledge through reflection on practice (Kember et al., 2001). The students had enrolled in postgraduate courses for health science professionals. Many of the students started with a set of related beliefs based on their experiences as passive recipients of knowledge presented didactically by a teacher. As the students were all practitioners in health science fields, the courses aimed to draw upon the students' experiences and practical knowledge, and develop their ability to reflect upon their practices. Their beliefs were exposed by employing various student-centred approaches to teaching and learning. This led to a period of discomfort for many of the students as in class they were expected to be active in constructing knowledge. Dissatisfaction with existing beliefs gradually developed as they came to recognize that their own experiences were of value and it was legitimate for them to determine which areas of knowledge were valuable to them. Eventually most students came to recognize that the more reflective approaches to teaching and learning were far more effective and appropriate for their professional roles.

Changes by CUHK Exemplary Teachers

The beginning of Chapter 7 notes that the majority of the teachers interviewed for this study accepted that their teaching had improved considerably over the years. About half described a developmental change which is important to the thesis of this chapter. These teachers admitted in the early part of their teaching careers they had tried to cover too much content. As their careers progressed they had adopted more student-centred approaches with the expectation that students would learn more.

The evidence of conceptions guiding teaching approaches suggests that the beliefs of these teachers are likely to have shifted over time away from the transmission pole of the spectrum towards more student-centred beliefs. Their initial beliefs were that teaching consisted of covering a substantial defined body of content, through presenting it to students. These beliefs shifted in time to focus more on what is learnt. They realized that it is not possible to equate what is taught with what is learnt.

> In the past, I was not methodical in my teaching and I was inclined to teach too much so that students would be too full to digest and assimilate what I had taught. I have then learnt that I should be more student-oriented. I have to somewhat readjust my expectation of students to a realistic level. (Francis Chan – Medicine and Therapeutics)

It would be instructive for enhancing the quality of teaching and learning if it were possible to deduce the reason for this shift in beliefs by many of the exemplary teachers. Eight of the interviewed teachers admitted in their interviews to have reduced the amount of content they tried to cover in favour of making sure that more fundamental aspects were thoroughly understood. The reasons for the change in attitude are not always clear from the interviews; this is not surprising as the teachers were not specifically asked about this, and may themselves have been unaware of why their beliefs changed.

What is clear is that the change happened over a period of time—there were no instant conversions. The most common influences appear to have been an accumulation of evidence of unintended outcomes in students' learning—or the lack of it. In some cases the evidence was in combination with feedback from students indicative of this problem. The teachers realized that covering more content does not lead to greater levels of learning. This combination of evidence of unintended outcomes and students' feedback served as a process for leading the teachers through the first two steps in conceptual change. They realized that their emphasis had been on covering content and became dissatisfied with the outcomes. This led to the possibility of moving on to adopt more student-centred beliefs.

Up till ten or so years ago, I used to teach very traditionally, delivering knowledge through lecturing. Standard model answers were provided by me, the teacher. I used to worry that my students came without enough knowledge of contemporary Chinese literature and that this would be a great chance for them to learn a lot in my lectures. I was eager to give them as much information as possible. I would speak incessantly and students in the past would be obedient enough to listen to it all. Even so, it doesn't mean that they had "digested" everything. Worse still, it is stuff that didn't belong to them—it is my understanding only. Education is not like that. It should stem from their own discovery. Knowledge is best assimilated when it is being discovered and becomes part of their lives. (Lo Wai Luen – Chinese Literature)

Potential Approaches to Changing Beliefs and Practices

If many of the interviewed teachers had attained exemplary status following a change in conceptions about teaching, it implies that there could be a general improvement in the quality of teaching and learning at CUHK if others were to shift their beliefs in a similar way. If the thesis of the previous chapter is accepted—that professors at reputable universities have an international culture—the same would be true in other universities around the world.

The discussion above suggests that promoting such a shift in beliefs is unlikely to be easy. The three-step conceptual change model suggests that existing beliefs of teachers will need to be exposed and challenged. The following sections consider various quality assurance or learning enhancement initiatives and speculate on whether they are able to provide the three steps in the conceptual change model. Whilst the examples are of initiatives here at CUHK, they all focus on the need to influence teachers' beliefs in any successful change process. We therefore believe that the discussion of these examples is relevant to a wide university audience.

We first examine a process for giving feedback to programmes on the level of their students' engagement with their studies. This process is now part of a new teaching and learning quality assurance plan for CUHK; this plan is considered as our second example. Finally, another component of the quality assurance scheme, a professional development course for teachers, is examined.

Programme-Level Feedback

The Student Engagement Project

For students to have a consistently high quality university experience, there needs to be a culture of teaching and learning across the whole institution. The process of assisting with this cultural change can be supported by using students' reports of their engagement in the programmes they study as a diagnostic tool for identifying effective teaching and learning strategies. Certain teaching practices are known to lead to high levels of student engagement (Chickering & Gamson, 1987). These practices include clearly planned courses, high expectations of students, high quality student–teacher contact, fostering cooperation among students, providing prompt feedback, and respect for diverse talents and ways of learning—indeed, the practices espoused by our exemplary teachers. Such practices are found in programmes that are designed to foster active learning and thus are likely to result in higher levels of student engagement. A suitable survey instrument for measuring student engagement needs to include items and scales seeking feedback about the students' perceptions of the level and quality of their engagement in these types of educational experiences.

During 2002, the Student Engagement Questionnaire (SEQ) was developed in order to measure student engagement. It was used during the academic years 2002–03 and 2003–04 across all undergraduate programmes at CUHK. It was then revised after extensive feedback from all faculties. Version 2 of the SEQ consists of 35 closed-ended items and two open-ended items. The closed items seek quantitative feedback on two types of information—eight scales measuring perceived development of capabilities (critical thinking, creative thinking, self-managed learning, adaptability, problem solving, communication skills, interpersonal skills and group work, and computer literacy) and nine scales seeking feedback on the teaching and learning environment (relating to: variety of learning activities, the level of interactivity with teachers, and with other students, the quality of the feedback received from teachers, if the assessment was relevant and guided learning, if the courses fitted together to make a coherent whole, and so forth). A five-point Likert scale is used to gather responses. Each scale of the SEQ has two or three items. Some examples of items are in Table 8.1.

Table 8.1. Sample SEQ Items

Scale	Example item
Critical thinking	I have developed my ability to make judgments about alternative perspectives
Self-managed learning	I feel that I can take responsibility for my own learning
Interpersonal skills and group work	I have learnt to become an effective team or group member
Active learning	Our teaching staff use a variety of teaching methods
Feedback to assist learning	There is sufficient feedback on activities and assignments to ensure that we learn from the work we do
Coherence of curriculum	I can see how courses fitted together to make a coherent programme of study for my major

It should be noted that the SEQ differs from normal micro-level course feedback questionnaires in that it is designed to collect data on students' holistic reflections of their experience at key stages in their studies and not just on recent experiences of a course. Each year the SEQ is administered to Year 1 and Year 3 students from half of the undergraduate major programmes (~25) in the seven faculties of CUHK. The remaining programmes are sampled the following academic year. Between 2,500–3,000 students are contacted by email and mail each year. The response rate is around 60%. Students can choose to complete the questionnaire either online or by mailing back the paper version. Both Chinese and English versions are available.

Feedback of the results from the project is sent to the chairperson of the relevant department or programme director for each of the selected programmes. The confidentiality of the data is stressed; this data is only given to each programme and not to the University administration. After this material had been sent out, individual chairs of the departments or her/his designate(s) are contacted for a meeting. During these meetings areas of teaching contributing to demonstrated strengths of the individual programmes are explored so that others might use the information as a model of best practice. We also discuss ways in which the feedback could be used in the processes of curriculum development and revision. The intended design for the Student Engagement Project fits the three-stage conceptual change model, as described in Table 8.2.

Table 8.2. The Student Engagement Project and the Three-stage Conceptual Change Model

Stage	Planned activity
Evidence of the need for change	The profiles produced for departments provide quantitative and qualitative explicit feedback on aspects of the programme. These profiles show programme performance in relation to the mean scale scores for the University as a whole. The data is presented diagrammatically, in numbers and in words.
Confronting the situation	The meeting that is scheduled is essential in ensuring that the report is not just filed. It should be noted that in the meeting positive features of the programme are celebrated and this assists the process of addressing more challenging issues.
Reconstruction of a new approach	Meetings are followed up and initiatives that address identified challenges are supported by workshops, training sessions and ongoing consultations. In a given programme the SEQ is administered every two years. This enables longitudinal tracking to support progressive improvements.

The feedback from the SEQ provides evidence of the need for change in the form of profiles reporting the programme's rating by its students on the development of eight capabilities and nine aspects of the teaching and learning environment. Comparison of these ratings with those of other departments suggests potential strengths and challenges for each programme. This information is supplemented with qualitative feedback from responses to two open-ended questions.

In the meetings the initial focus is often on the strengths of the programme. An intention of this discussion is to identify forms of good practice in teaching and curriculum design so that other departments can learn from these.

The meetings also try to focus on challenges, with the aim of jointly devising strategies to address them. This aim has been met most successfully in programmes where the profiles have generally been on the positive side. In such cases the departments concerned have often been quite keen to identify relative weaknesses and determine how to deal with them.

Where the profiles have been generally on the negative side, there has usually been less progress in persuading departments to confront the issues. However, it has to be said clearly that there have been two or three exceptions to this generalization when departments have tried to comprehensively address strongly negative feedback from their students.

This finding can be readily explained by the analytical framework introduced in the previous chapter. If the conceptions of teaching in a department are predominately teacher-centred, then the curriculum design and approach to teaching is highly likely to follow logically and coherently from that predominant belief, and be didactic in nature. Unfortunately, such conceptions and practices tend to be associated with less desirable learning outcomes. In dealing with negative feedback from students, departments like these need to address the philosophy on which their teaching and course design are based. Earlier sections have shown how difficult it is for individuals to change deep-seated conceptions. Changing philosophies entrenched within a department is even more difficult as a significant number of teachers need to begin the process of changing beliefs and practice at the same time.

As change on this scale does not occur frequently, it is sensible to adopt an incremental approach where small challenges are confronted and acted upon first. While this may not result in rapid fundamental changes to beliefs and practice across the whole department, such an approach can, over time, build up an evidence base that becomes a "turning point" for the department. Some examples of interventions that have been useful in this small scale approach are presented in Table 8.3.

Table 8.3. Interventions Resulting From the Student Engagement Project

Issue identified by the SEQ	Intervention focus
Unengaging large group teaching	Seminars on active learning and presentation skills
Low interactivity in tutorials	Suggestions for group work and facilitating communication. All teaching assistants at CUHK undergo mandatory professional development courses; these are tailored for each department.
Assessment inconsistent with course goals	Developing a matrix of learning outcomes and assessment tasks as a stimulus for discussion about how best to write appropriate assessment tasks
Student concerns with professional development	Exploration of strategies for lifelong learning, often using a case-based approach

University-Level Quality Assurance

The CUHK Integrated Framework

In Chapter 1 we began this book by noting the educational quality literature that highlights the centrality of beliefs in the organization of effective quality assurance schemes. In this final chapter we return again to the same theme by examining a new approach to quality assurance that CUHK is about to implement. We will consider to what extent this plan fits the model of conceptual change. Is it likely to engender an attitude of forced compliance or could it be a power for transformative change in the beliefs about teaching and learning at CUHK? What are the key factors that might determine the nature of any changes that are effected?

The "Integrated Framework for Curriculum Development and Review" has been developed in order to assist programmes and departments gather evidence that will be useful in tracking and reflecting on their achievements and their challenges in teaching and learning. The framework is based on the principle of curriculum alignment (Biggs, 2003) which seeks evidence for the coherence between content, desired learning outcomes, learning activities (including assessment strategies), and evaluative feedback. The main elements of the framework are:

- Clear planning of programmes and their constituent courses. Course and programme planning guides have been written.
- Internal course reviews every three years. A guide for course review has been written.
- A programme self-evaluation review every six years. A guide for programme review has been written. A formal programme review panel examines the effectiveness of the programme team's self-evaluation. The panel's report leads to an action plan to deal with challenges and improve the quality of teaching and learning within the programme. The programme external examiner is involved in the programme review and thus the role of the external examiner has been broadened from its previous main focus on student assessment tasks and marks.
- Professional development for teaching assistants and for teachers relatively new to CUHK at the rank of Instructor and Assistant Professor.

Just how likely is it that the Integrated Framework will facilitate change across the University? Earlier in this chapter, the persistence of beliefs was discussed with reference to teaching physics and economics. When teachers taught Newtonian mechanics or supply and demand without managing to change students' conceptions of these concepts, the students found it difficult to apply the concepts to realistic examples. A parallel can be seen with the introduction of the Integrated Framework. It has been introduced by a process which has, as yet, not included the University's teachers in the three phases for conceptual change. A consultative process with faculties has been enabled through the Senate Committee on Teaching and Learning and its associated Working Parties. Pragmatically, this has involved only a small number of CUHK teachers, and so most teachers are unclear about the reasons for the policy change.

The Integrated Framework arose from ongoing work and existing policies at CUHK. However, there is no doubt that the final articulation of the Integrated Framework was crystallized by a recent report made by the University Grants Committee (UGC) as part of its periodic teaching and learning quality reviews of all Hong Kong universities.

As the CUHK teaching staff have not, in the main, been involved in the three steps for conceptual change, their beliefs about teaching quality assurance are unlikely to have changed. There is no evidence of widespread dissatisfaction with the existing devolved responsibility for quality and, as a consequence, it is likely that many teachers do not truly see the need for a centralized review system. They nevertheless accept that its introduction is inevitable because it has been supported by the UGC, the University's main source of funding.

When quality assurance measures are introduced as required measures there is a tendency for passive compliance or avoidance on the part of those who have not taken the need to heart. Bryman, Haslam, & Webb (1994) examined the imposed introduction of staff appraisal into U.K. universities. They concluded that appraisal was widely disliked by both appraisers and appraisees and felt that the operation of the schemes could best be characterized as "procedural compliance". They also found scant evidence of the expected benefits of appraisal. As this effect is well known, it is important that CUHK avoid the same trap.

Programme Reviews

How the intended design for the reviews associated with the Integrated Framework fits the three-stage conceptual change model is shown in Table 8.4.

Table 8.4. The Integrated Framework and the Three-stage Conceptual Change Model

Stage	Planned activity
Evidence of the need for change	The course and programme review guides outline how quality assurance evidence can be collected. The data for this evidence can include a number of sources such as questionnaires, student panels and forums, reflections of teachers, assessment results, and peer review from colleagues.
Confronting the situation	A consideration of the programme review report by a meeting of the programme review panel with teachers responsible for the programme is integral to the process.
Reconstruction of a new approach	The reviews are cyclical and this encourages progressive trials and evaluation.

The review process will not succeed unless the evidence programmes need to present is sufficiently diagnostic of teaching and learning in the programme. Most of this evidence will need to come from the students in the programme, as they are in the best position to assess the impact on their learning, which is what education is all about. It is also important that the evidence, and the evaluation on which it is based, is multifaceted, in terms of both the factors examined and sources of data.

It is widely accepted that teaching is a multidimensional phenomenon (Marsh, 1987); consequently, evaluation of teaching needs to consider a wide range of factors in the teaching and learning environment at both course and programme level. If evaluation data like this is available, a diagnosis can be made of strengths and aspects which need attention. Relying on one or two overall ratings does not give this diagnostic information.

Assuming that the implementation of the Integrated Framework is successful in requiring the collection and presentation of diagnostic data, the most sensitive of the three phases then needs to be addressed. The framework incorporates the standard approach to "confronting the situation" which is a meeting between a review panel and representatives of the responsible programme team.

The experience of these meetings may partially resemble the meetings of the Student Engagement Project. Where the diagnostic information is largely positive the review meeting is likely to be a harmonious discussion of how best to deal with the limited number of outstanding issues. Review panels faced with programmes with overwhelmingly negative evidence will find the process more challenging. Firstly, the departments concerned may be reluctant to put forward the evidence. Secondly, it will be more difficult to address underlying issues in a manner which is credible to the staff of the department because the recommendations for change are likely to be inconsistent with the predominant beliefs about teaching and learning. However, if review panels do not make recommendations for changes in programmes with challenges, the Integrated Framework will lack credibility. If the only departments making changes are those with positive feedback, the UGC is unlikely to be convinced of the effectiveness of the quality assurance measures.

For the review process to successfully lead to the reconstruction of a new approach, there will be a need for staff development and curriculum reconstruction within departments. This will need to be tailored for each department so as to address the specific recommendations made for its programme.

The crux of the success of this strategy will be whether departments see that an evidence-based approach to quality assurance brings real benefits in terms of student satisfaction and improved student learning outcomes. The administrative load of the reviews needs to be minimized through careful design of processes and supportive guidelines to departments. Being helpful but not prescriptive; being rigorous but not nit-picking; providing expert advice but not preempting local wisdom: these are some of the tensions to be negotiated in implementing the reviews associated with the Integrated Framework.

Professional Development for Individuals

"Becoming an Excellent Teacher" Course

This course for teachers who are relatively new to teaching at CUHK aims at enabling teachers to reflect on their own practice as part of a process of conceptual change. For teachers at the rank of Instructor and Assistant Professor this course is mandatory. The course explicitly includes vignettes about the exemplary teachers whose voices are heard in this book and is titled the "Becoming an excellent teacher" course. Using an approach strongly based on curriculum alignment, there are sessions on planning courses, teaching larger classes, teaching smaller classes, devising appropriate assessment and obtaining feedback for evaluation. The way in which the course fits the three-stage process is described in Table 8.5.

Table 8.5. The Excellent Teacher Course and the Three-stage Conceptual Change Model

Stage	Planned activity
Evidence of the need for change	Activities in the course are based on the existing course outlines and assessment items used by teachers in the course. When a mismatch exists between current practice and an aligned curriculum, it will become fairly obvious.
Confronting the situation	The use of vignettes of excellent teachers in the course may disturb some transmissive teachers as it shows that teachers judged exemplary have different practices to their own. This includes teachers from all faculties as the principles of excellent teaching are consistent and there are examples from each faculty showing practices very different to transmission.
Reconstruction of a new approach	The assignment for the group is a group project where each group takes on teaching about a particular form of teaching. The method of teaching is expected to be congruent with the form of teaching. Teachers thus are exposed to forms of teaching such as case-based and problem-based learning, role plays, debates, field work, peer tutoring and appropriate uses of web-assisted learning. Peer assessment is used within the group project. This assignment has been designed to give teachers some experiential base for enhancements in their teaching. In addition, a community of practice (Wegner, 1998) is built up as far as possible during the course, so that individual teachers' isolation is reduced and each person has a range of colleagues with shared understanding of the principles of excellent teaching.

The course begins by drawing from the teachers a consensus about the capabilities needed by CUHK graduates. The course then seeks to prompt reflection on whether teachers' approaches to course plans, assessment items and feedback from students are consistent with the aims of their courses and the programme level goals implied by the capabilities.

While the design of the course is appropriate for drawing out evidence of inconsistencies between aims and practices, to what extent it will succeed in confronting beliefs is open to question. The review by Wideen, Mayer-Smith and Moon (1998), cited earlier in this chapter, concluded that most teacher training programmes had limited impact on the beliefs of the trainee teachers. It did, however, note that those based, like the CUHK course, on reflection-on-practice were more successful. However, this review was of school teacher education programmes, which last for at least one year and are often for three or four years. The CUHK course is just 12 hours in duration. If teacher educators find it hard to influence the beliefs of trainee school teachers over a period of years, it is optimistic to think this can be done in a matter of a few hours, however well designed the course.

It is too early to see whether the "Becoming an excellent teacher" course will impact significantly on individuals and, ultimately, on departmental and university culture. In Chapter 7 the ways in which our exemplary teachers handled the tension of meeting research and teaching demands are explored. Our "new" teachers will need to face this tension. Depending on the departmental context, suggestions for change that newcomers bring can be warmly welcomed or regarded with suspicion. The success of the "Becoming an excellent teacher" course may well depend on the success of implementation of the whole Integrated Framework.

General Principles for Quality Assurance

These recent initiatives at CUHK have drawn inspiration and direction from the principles of excellent teaching discussed in this book. The Integrated Framework is designed to support CUHK teaching in seeking evidence of educational quality, reflecting on it and then moving into cycles of continuous improvement. The framework sets out review processes at both programme and course level and prescribes some mandatory professional development. We have outlined two components of the Integrated Framework in more detail; namely, one mechanism for obtaining programme-level feedback using the Student Engagement Questionnaire, and a scheme for widespread professional development of teachers. Are there any common principles which can summarize the approach taken within these components of the Integrated Framework? In order to be effective, quality assurance policies need to have acceptance within the organization. It is our experience over the past two years that acceptance of change within CUHK requires an approach to teaching and learning that is both scholarly and pragmatic. An economic rationalist approach to quality assurance with a dominant focus on funding is not congruent with the principles of excellent teaching endorsed by the designers of the Integrated Framework. The logic of an aligned curriculum and the student-centred focus advocated by our exemplary teachers indicate strongly that CUHK's quality assurance policy and processes need to have this scholarly, pragmatic approach. This approach implies that quality assurance needs to:

- be based on student experience. Student learning outcomes are one keystone of an aligned curriculum and students' outcomes in terms of discipline knowledge and skills, capability development, and attitudes need to be central to the appraisal of quality.

- facilitate changes to teaching and learning which are practical. Change needs to be feasible and incremental success is a strong motivator to continue the process of seeking improvement.

- be validated by actual projects which are monitored in an ongoing fashion within the institution. Collecting an ongoing and growing base of evidence of student learning is the only scholarly approach to take in an academic institution.

The Exemplary Teacher Awards

To end the book it seems appropriate to return to the origins of the material on which it is based—the CUHK Vice-Chancellor's Exemplary Teacher Award scheme. This in itself can be seen as an initiative to enhance the quality of teaching and learning. The rationale for such schemes is normally that of enhancing the status of teaching. Universities have been criticized for recognizing and rewarding research more than teaching. Schemes which demonstrate that excellence in teaching is valued are seen as addressing the balance.

Such schemes have been criticized. An obvious potential danger is that the rewards and recognition accorded to the award-winning teachers are perceived as being markedly inferior to the way in which outstanding researchers are celebrated. There is a danger of award schemes actually undermining the value of teaching if it is perceived that successful researchers are promoted while excellent teachers receive a certificate.

A further criticism of teaching award schemes can be found in *Teaching the Chinese learner*. The quotation from Biggs and Watkins (2001) is given below at some length. The following text considers the applicability of the critique for the CUHK exemplary teacher scheme:

> In many Western universities, and in the University Grants Committee guidelines in Hong Kong, an institutional performance indicator of good teaching is whether or not a distinguished teacher award system is in place. If it is, the institution may be seen to be doing its bit for good teaching. This is missing the point, because other teachers are then free to continue doing what they always

have been doing. Unless there are good and well-resourced staff development facilities also in place, and the distinguished teachers are required to share their expertise in general staff development exercises, as in the Chinese and Japanese examples, the message of such award systems can be quite counterproductive. What is left is a conception of the excellent teacher as the Oscar winning performer, not the constructivist—and Confucian—view of the teacher as a facilitator of learning (p. 280).

The "Chinese and Japanese examples" refer to model school teacher schemes in those countries. Cortazzi and Jin (2001) described the Chinese version. The awards winners are selected through competitions in the form of demonstration lessons. As the audiences can be large, the competitions themselves have a modelling effect. The award-winning teachers then take a senior role in lesson planning. Plans are discussed at weekly meetings with advice from the experienced model teachers. It is also common for the distinguished teachers to act as observers in classes taught by others. Post-lesson feedback and discussion can lead to constructive reflection on the teaching.

Using the exemplary university teachers in precisely the same way would hardly be feasible. University teachers tend to be less open to observation of, or input into, the planning of their teaching. The additional roles of the model school teachers would be seen by university teachers as making the award into a penalty rather than a prize.

This book was seen as a way of enabling the award winners to share their expertise without inordinate commitment of time to staff development exercises. Material from the book can be used in workshops and courses. The book itself can be read by teachers of CUHK. As the principles of good teaching are drawn from their colleagues, more notice is likely to be taken than of treatises written elsewhere.

Suggestions for Changing the Exemplary Teaching Award Scheme

The spirit of this book is one of reflection and reconstruction and it is fitting that the book ends with suggestions for further enhancement of this award scheme. The analysis in this book suggests that the selections have been appropriate ones—we indeed have a growing community of exemplary teachers—even though the selection procedures are not clear. However, this lack of clarity does not serve the scheme well and provides grounds for detractors. One way to enhance the scheme is to take the first two of the three principles stated above for successful quality assurance and apply them to the exemplary teaching award scheme.

An Award Based on Student Experience

Student evaluation data are important in all the various faculty award schemes at CUHK. It is suggested that greater student input to the decision-making may result in a more valid system. Course evaluation profiles from student feedback are already considered in all the faculty selection schemes. It is therefore important that this data be credible as selection data for excellence in teaching. If student experience is to remain a lynchpin of quality assurance, then course evaluation questionnaires need to be firmly connected to the principles of excellent teaching. Only then can this data be truly useful in the exemplary teaching award scheme.

In addition, active inclusion of students in all the faculty panels which decide on these awards may improve the transparency of the process and lead to greater acceptance of the choices by all members of the University.

In most departments at CUHK, department chairs are the only people who can see complete course evaluations; in some departments summary statistics of the quantitative date are not even provided. In such cases individual teachers have no idea how their own teaching may compare with that of other teachers in the department and this can reinforce a feeling of isolation. The focus on student feedback can raise the profile of teachers who achieve well in this arena. It can also reinforce the importance of careful reflection on the meaning of this student feedback data. Active discussion about how course evaluation feedback from students can support excellence in teaching within a department occurs in many departments. A stronger emphasis on the student voice may strengthen this reflective practice across the University.

An Award Based on Demonstrable Practical Enhancements in Teaching and Learning

In some quarters, it is thought that the more paperwork and more outside recommendations a candidate offers, the better the chance of obtaining an exemplary teaching award. Such a view contributes considerably to the skepticism with which the award is viewed by some. If the criteria for the award are based quite explicitly on principles of excellent teaching, then candidates can be asked to provide evidence that demonstrates how their teaching practice relates to these principles. This again brings us to the need for sound evaluation of teaching within courses and programmes. Only with this approach of articulating criteria based on clear principles, and then using a clear evidence basis for selection, will the award scheme be widely accepted. Again, this suggestion is aimed at grounding the award in the practice that it celebrates— teaching that is aligned to the principles of excellent teaching.

This clearly highlights the need to have clear and explicit criteria for the selection of exemplary teachers. Now that these principles of excellent teaching have been articulated, these could form the base for drawing up the criteria against which candidates can be judged.

The 18 exemplary teachers of The Chinese University of Hong Kong interviewed in this study are united in their adherence to and exemplification of the 17 principles of excellent teaching outlined in this book. It is offered to all teachers of this University and elsewhere as a grounded and consistent account of excellence in teaching.

Profiles of Contributors (2004)

David AHLSTROM

 I am currently an Associate Professor of Management at CUHK, where I teach courses in strategic management, management of technology, and global strategy and international relations for global managers. I also teach a course in the Chinese University Faculty of Medicine that helps students prepare for the (United Kingdom) Royal College of Medicine examination in public health. I was awarded the first University-wide Exemplary Teaching Award in CUHK in 1999, and more recently the CUHK Faculty of Business Teaching Award in 2004. While at New York University, I was awarded the NYU–Stern School of Business Outstanding Teacher Award (in 1995). My graduate degrees are in management and international business and I also have a degree in history. My research examines firm turnaround in East Asia, the nature of entrepreneurship and venture capital in Asia, and strategic alliance partner selection preferences by firms based in transition economies. I have published 40 peer-reviewed articles in a variety of management and entrepreneurship journals. I also worked in the Asia-Pacific region in the computer field before teaching in the United States and Hong Kong.

Andrew Chi Fai CHAN

I am a Professor in the Department of Marketing and currently the Director of the EMBA Program at CUHK. I obtained my MBA from The University of California at Berkeley, my BBA and PhD from CUHK. Before I started my teaching career, I worked for the Bank of America and the IBM World Trade Corporation. I have taught various subjects in marketing: advertising management, sales management, marketing research, marketing management, consumer behaviour, customer relationship management, and strategic marketing. My interaction with students and alumni does  not only occur in class, but also occurs via social gatherings, dinners/lunches, seminars, and so forth. My research areas cover strategic marketing, cyber marketing, cross-cultural marketing, consumerism, and business negotiation. As I am a strong believer of "relevancy in teaching", I am greatly interested in doing research that can enhance my teaching and consultative service.

Francis K. L. CHAN

After I completed my secondary education at St. Francis Xavier's College, I studied medicine at CUHK and graduated with honors in 1988. I studied at the University of Calgary as a Croucher Foundation Research Fellow in 1993 after completing my residency training in Hong Kong. In 1997, I was appointed Lecturer in the Department of Medicine and Therapeutics of CUHK. Based on my research work on animal liver transplantation, I was awarded the degree of Doctor of Medicine by CUHK in 1998. My research focuses on common gastrointestinal diseases including peptic ulcers, and gastric and colorectal cancers. I was appointed Senior Lecturer and Reader in 2000 and 2003, respectively. Currently, I am a fellow of a number of professional colleges in Hong Kong, London, Edinburgh, Ireland, and the United States. Besides teaching medical students, I serve as associate editor and editorial board member in several international gastroenterology journals.

CHAN Hung Kan

Before I started teaching at CUHK in August 1986, I was a secondary school teacher and an editor. I am now Chair and Professor of the Department of Chinese Language and Literature, and have been teaching for 17 years. The subjects that I teach include "Introduction to Chinese etymology", "Chinese writing", and "Study of Cantonese and its application". My research interest surrounds Chinese semasiology, Chinese etymology and Chinese grammar. I believe that teaching should be student-oriented, tempered by students' different abilities. If a teacher is accommodating and sincere to students, they will enjoy learning and respect their teacher.

Gregory CHENG

I was born in Hong Kong and completed secondary school at St. Joseph's College. In 1971 I went abroad and studied in Canada, and obtained MD and PhD degrees at the University of Toronto, specializing in haematology, transfusion medicine and oncology. I returned to work in Hong Kong in 1992, at the University of Hong Kong. I joined CUHK in 1997 as a Professor II in Department of Medicine and Therapeutics. I am a Fellow of the Royal College of Physicians of Canada and the Hong Kong Academy of Medicine. I believe that teaching should be student-oriented. I enjoy teaching and one of my greatest joys is students enjoying my teaching.

Gordon Wai Hung CHEUNG

I started my teaching profession at CUHK in January 1994 and am currently Professor at the Department of Management and Associate Dean of the Faculty of Business Administration. My research interests include structural equation modelling, cross-cultural comparisons and performance appraisal. I was elected as an Executive Officer and the Chair of the Research Methods Division at the Academy of Management for a five-year term starting 2003. I believe that students at CUHK are very brilliant and the task of a professor is to inspire and motivate them to perform at their best. I have trained many case competition teams in recent years and they have performed outstandingly in many international case competitions, defeating students from the most prestigious business schools in the world. My recent task is to develop a system of soft skills training for the business students, which complements the formal education they receive in the classrooms.

CHU Ming Chung

Professor, Department of Physics at CUHK. In 1979, I moved to the States after finishing secondary school in Hong Kong. I ended up at Caltech, where I stayed for twelve years altogether, first as a student (both undergraduate and graduate) and then as a Senior Research Fellow. Ironically, coming back to Hong Kong in 1995 was a cultural shock for myself, but I quickly adapted to the family-like atmosphere at CUHK, where I realized that a positive teacher–student relationship is one of the most important elements in a quality education. My current research interest is in astrophysics and cosmology, which must have grown from my fondness for star-gazing since I was young. I continue to be awed by the beauty of nature. My prime motivation to excel in teaching is probably my desire to share this excitement with young kids.

FAN Jianqing

I am a Professor of Statistics at CUHK and was the chairman of the department from 2000 to 2003. After obtaining my PhD degree from the University of California at Berkeley, I was assistant, associate and full professor at the University of North Carolina at Chapel Hill and the University of California at Los Angeles. I have taught different kinds and levels of statistics courses with enthusiasm over the last 14 years at various institutions. I speak both Mandarin and English and this adds additional experiences to my teaching in Hong Kong. My research focuses on the development of statistical theory and methodology with emphasis on the applications to financial econometrics, risk management and computational biology. My research was recognized by The 2000 COPSS President's Award for the most outstanding statistician under age 40 by five major international statistical societies. My research was ranked on the top ten most highly cited mathematical scientists between 1991–2001 and 1993–2003 by the Science Watch.

David KEMBER

I left the United Kingdom shortly after completing my PhD. My academic career was a journey, through Fiji, Papua New Guinea and Australia, to eventually become marooned in Hong Kong for the past 16 years. There was an accompanying transition from a Lecturer in Chemistry to a Professor of Learning Enhancement, which resulted from a developing interest in teaching and learning and a waxing commitment to chemistry. My work in teaching development has always had a research-based orientation and I have been one of the pioneers in championing quality enhancement through action research. I have been a significant contributor to the now well-known body of research on the Chinese learner.

Patrick S. Y. LAU

I majored in biology as an undergraduate at CUHK, and completed my PgDE, MA(Ed) in Counselling and PhD at the same university. After being a teacher and principal of secondary schools in Hong Kong, I had a desire to promote humanism in teacher education. In 1990, therefore, I joined Hong Kong Baptist University as an Assistant Professor and was later appointed the Course Planning Committee Chairperson and the Course Leader of their Postgraduate Diploma in Education Programme. I returned to teach in the Educational Psychology Department of the CUHK in 1999. My research relates primarily to teacher burnout,

school guidance and adaptation of newly arrived students from the Mainland. Albeit the changes in positions, I firmly believe teaching is a way of life. I believe in genuineness, empathy and respect, so that both students and I can grow perpetually. I treasure this growing journey and am sure I always will.

John Chi Kin LEE

I am a Professor in the Department of Curriculum and Instruction and currently Dean of the Faculty of Education at CUHK. Following undergraduate study at the University of Hong Kong I gained a professional teaching qualification with DipEd with Distinctions, MA (Ed) and a PhD at CUHK. I also studied for a year at the University of Oxford in the United Kingdom. Having gained experience as a secondary school geography teacher I was appointed to a Lectureship in the Sir Robert Black College of Education and then moved on to a Lectureship at CUHK in the early 1990s. I have a longstanding research interest in geographical and environmental education, the school curriculum, teaching and learning. More recently I have been actively involved in leading a number of externally funded projects on school effectiveness and improvement and university–school partnerships. I have a substantial publications record including authored and coauthored books, research reports, book chapters and articles in a range of international and regional refereed journals.

Kenneth W. Y. LEUNG

Born and brought up in Hong Kong, I completed my undergraduate study in journalism, worked as a reporter for United Press International (UPI) for two years before I pursued my MA and PhD programmes at the University of Minnesota (United States). I returned to teach at Hong Kong Baptist College for four years, served as a visiting professor for one year at Malone College in Ohio, and have been at CUHK since 1983. I have taught practical courses in journalistic writing, theory and research courses at both undergraduate as well postgraduate levels. My recent interest in both  teaching and research is media ethics and law. I coauthored with Prof. Johannes Chan of the University of Hong Kong the first and only book in media law in Hong Kong. Currently I am working on one RGC-funded project on libel litigations in Hong Kong, and another Chiang Ching Kuo Foundation-funded project on a communication campaign that changes traditional Chinese values in Taiwan.

LEUNG Sing Fai

I practise in a very specialized branch of medicine (radiation oncology: using radiation to treat cancer) but I adopt a nonspecialist perspective in teaching undergraduates. I research mainly on one specific disease (nasopharynx cancer) but I teach on a broad spectrum of medical problems. Some of my patients are inflicted with incurable illness and I hope to explore some of the positive aspect of their illness with them. All of my students are endowed with a lot of blessings and treasures and I hope to rediscover with them some of the greatest attractions in medicine and in life. I joined the University in 1989 and I have 15 years' experience of learning to teach.

Soung C. LIEW

I am currently Professor and Director of the Area of Excellence in Information Technology at CUHK. I teach various subjects related to computer networking and network software design and programming. Before coming to CUHK in 1993, I was a Member of Technical Staff at Bellcore (now Telcordia), New Jersey, where I was engaged in broadband network research. My current research interests include wireless networking, Internet protocols, and multimedia communications. Besides academic activities, I have also been active in the industry. I cofounded two technology start-ups in Internet software, and have served as a consultant to many other companies and industrial organizations. I am currently consultant for the Hong Kong Applied Science and Technology Research Institute, helping to formulate R&D directions and strategies in the areas of wireless Internetworking, applications and services. I am a firm believer of the inseparability of university teaching and research, that good teachers tend to be good researchers, and vice versa.

LO Wai Luen

My family came from Panyu, Guangdong Province and I was born in Hong Kong. I publish under the pen-names 小思 ("Xiao Si") and 明川 ("Ming Chuan"). After I graduated from the Department of Chinese Language and Literature of the New Asia College, CUHK, I taught in a secondary school for some years before working as a Research Associate at the Institute for Research in Humanities at Kyoto University, Japan. In 1981, I was awarded an MPhil from the University of Hong Kong. My teaching at the CUHK with the Department of Chinese Language and Literature started in 1979 and I received the Vice-Chancellor's Exemplary Teaching Award in 2000. Since my retirement in July 2002, I have been an honorary research fellow and director for the Hong Kong Literature Research Centre at CUHK. My research specialty is in Chinese modern and contemporary literature, creative writing and the development of Hong Kong literature. My publications include《豐子愷漫畫選繹》、《承教小記》、《香港故事》、《香港家書》and《夜讀閃念》and so forth. In 2003, I was honored to receive the Outstanding Educator Award of the Hong Kong Institute of Education.

John Chi Shing LUI

I was born in Hong Kong. I received my PhD in computer science from UCLA. After graduation, I joined the IBM Almaden Research Laboratory, San Jose, and participated in various research and development projects on file systems and parallel I/O architectures. I later joined the Department of Computer Science and Engineering at CUHK. For the past several summers, I have been a visiting professor in computer science departments at UCLA, Columbia University, University of Maryland at College Park, Purdue University, University of Massachusetts at Amherst and Universit degli Studi di Torino in Italy. I am an affiliated member of the Integrated Media Systems Center (IMSC) at University of Southern California (USC). Currently, I am leading a group of research students in doing some interesting and exciting networking research. My research interests span across system work and theory/mathematics. My current research interests are in theoretical and applied topics in data networks, distributed multimedia systems, network security, OS design issues and mathematical optimization and performance evaluation theory. I received the CUHK Vice-Chancellor's Exemplary Teaching Award in 2001. I am an associate editor of the Performance Evaluation Journal, member of ACM, a senior member of IEEE and an elected member in the IFIP WG 7.3. My personal interests include films and general reading.

Rosa MA

Born and bred in Hong Kong, I was educated to A-Level locally. After leaving school, I started a tutorial centre teaching a variety of subjects to children aged 6 to 14. This experience inspired me to study psychology and its applications to learning at the University of Wales, Bangor (United Kingdom). Upon graduation, I conducted research into various forms of learning in different contexts, in particular, developmental psychology and entrepreneurship. I was awarded a doctoral fellowship by the University of Durham to study enterprise education, investigating the development of greater insights into knowledge and enterprising behaviours in young people. My research work over the past 13 years has consolidated my role as an educational developer/consultant and has given me a wide area of expertise. On this project I was a Visiting Scholar working with Carmel and David.

Gordon MATHEWS

I grew up in the United States, graduated from Yale University in 1978, and spent the 1980s in Japan before going to graduate school and then coming to Hong Kong. I've been in the Department of Anthropology at CUHK for the past ten years, and teach courses such as "Anthropological theory", "Meanings of life", "Globalization and culture", and "Language, symbols and society". I've written two books, *What makes life worth living? How Japanese and Americans make sense of their lives* (1996) and *Global culture/individual identity: Searching for home in the cultural supermarket* (2000) and edited two more, *Consuming Hong Kong* (2001) and *Japan's changing generations: Are young people creating a new society?* (2004). I've also made four jazz CDs as half of the Hong Kong Silicon Orchestra, and chaired the Hong Kong Anthropological Society for the past three years. But teaching is still the most important and the most fun thing I do in my life!

Carmel McNAUGHT

Professor of Learning Enhancement at CUHK. I have had three decades of work in eight universities in Australasia, southern Africa and Britain. I started my academic life in chemistry, but found the issues of learning science in a second language much more engaging, and so my PhD work examines the Zulu-English linguistic interface. During the 1990s much of my work was as a designer and evaluator in multimedia and web-based education projects. I consider that I am privileged to have had such a breadth of experience and this leaves me well placed to work across a variety of discipline areas. The changes in my own academic life across discipline boundaries, countries and cultures have led to my current research interests in the evaluation of innovation in higher education and understanding the broader implementation of the use of technology in higher education.

Allan WALKER

I began my career as a primary school teacher in a small town in Australia before becoming principal of an Aboriginal school located in the "Bush". My transition to academia began when I travelled to the United States to complete my Masters and PhD in educational leadership and policy analysis. During my studies I developed a keen interest in leadership learning and development, an interest which has stayed with me till today. Upon completing my studies, and following a short sojourn back in the classroom, I took up my first job in higher education at what became Nanyang Technological University in Singapore. I moved to my second in Australia three or so years later, and then accepted a position at CUHK in 1994. My research over the years has focused on understanding and developing leadership and its relationship to school improvement in different cultural contexts.

ZHANG Shuzhong

I graduated from the Department of Mathematics at Fudan University in 1984, and obtained my PhD degree from Tinbergen Institute, Erasmus University, in 1991. After that I worked as a faculty member at Department of Econometrics, University of Groningen (1991–1993), and Econometric Institute, Erasmus University (1993–1999). Since 1999, I have been with the Department of Systems Engineering & Engineering Management at CUHK. My main research interests include the use of quantitative methods for solving problems arising from engineering, management and economics. I was ranked number 6 among top 40 economists in The Netherlands in 1999, and in the same year I received the Erasmus University Research Prize. In 2003, I shared the SIAM Outstanding Paper Prize with my colleagues David Yao and Xunyu Zhou. The most satisfying result of a teacher, I believe, is to get students interested and to share the desire and enthusiasm towards the discovery of knowledge.

References

American Society for Quality. Glossary. Retrieved February 11, 2006, from http://www.asq.org/info/glossary/q.html

Bain, K. (2004). *What the best college teachers do.* Cambridge, MA: Harvard University Press.

Ballantyne, R., Bain, J., & Packer, J. (1997). *Reflecting on university teaching: Academics' stories.* Canberra: Australian Government Publishing Service.

Barnes, M. W., & Patterson, R. H. (1988, August). *Using teaching evaluation results to plan departmental strategies to accomplish the institutional mission.* Paper presented at the Annual Meeting of the Society for College and University Planning, Toronto.

Becher, T. (1989). *Academic tribes and territories: Intellectual enquiry and the cultures of disciplines.* Milton Keynes, U.K.: SRHE and Open University Press.

Beidler, P. G. (1997). What makes a good teacher? In J. K. Roth (Ed.), *Inspiring teaching. Carnegie Professors of the Year speak* (pp. 2–12). Bolton, MA: Anker Publisher Company, Inc.

Bennett, N. (1976). *Teaching styles and pupil progress.* London: Open Books.

Biggs, J. B. (2003). *Teaching for quality learning at university: What the student does* (2nd ed.). Buckingham, U.K.: Society for Research into Higher Education & Open University Press.

Biggs, J. B., & Watkins, D. (2001). Insights into teaching the Chinese learner. In D. Watkins & J. B. Biggs (Eds.), *Teaching the Chinese learner: Psychological and pedagogical perspectives* (pp. 277–300). Hong Kong and Melbourne: Comparative Education Research Centre, University of Hong Kong & the Australian Council for Educational Research.

Biglan, A. (1973). Relationships between subject matter characteristics and the structure and output of university departments. *Journal of Applied Psychology, 57*(3), 204–213.

Brady, L. (1990). *Curriculum development* (3rd ed.). Sydney: Prentice Hall.

Bruner, J. (1990). *Acts of meaning.* Cambridge, MA: Harvard University Press.

Bryman, A., Haslam, C., & Webb, A. (1994). Performance appraisal in U.K. universities: A case of procedural compliance? *Assessment and Evaluation in Higher Education, 19*(3), 175–187.

Burman, E., & Parker, I. (1993). Against discursive imperialism, empiricism and constructionism: Thirty-two problems with discourse analysis. In E. Burman & I. Parker (Eds.), *Discourse analytic research: Repertoires and readings of texts in action* (pp. 155–175). London: Routledge.

Burr, V. (1995). *An introduction to social constructivism.* London: Routledge.

Carless, D. (1998). Managing systematic curriculum change: A critical analysis of Hong Kong's target oriented curriculum initiative. In P. Simpson & P. Morris (Eds.), *Curriculum and assessment for Hong Kong: Two components, one system* (pp. 223–242). Hong Kong: Open University of Hong Kong Press.

Cashin, W. E. (1995). Students do rate different academic fields differently. In M. Theall & J. Franklin (Eds.), *Student ratings of instruction: Issues for improving practice* (pp. 113–121). San Francisco: Jossey-Bass.

Champagne, A. B., Gunstone, R. F., & Klopfer, L. E. (1985). Effecting changes in cognitive structures among physics students. In L. H. T. West & A. L. Pines (Eds.), *Cognitive structure and conceptual change* (pp. 163–187). New York: Academic Press.

Cheung, P. C., & Lau, S. (1985). Self-esteem: Its relationship to family and school social environments among Chinese adolescents. *Youth and Society, 16*(4), 438–456.

Chickering, A. W., & Gamson, Z. F. (1987). Seven principles for good practice in undergraduate education. *AAHE Bulletin, 39*(7), 3–7.

Cohen, L., & Manion, L. (1994). *Research methods in education* (4th ed.). London: Routledge.

Cortazzi, M., & Jin, L. (2001). Large classes in China: "Good" teachers and interaction. In D. Watkins & J. B. Biggs (Eds.), *Teaching the Chinese learner: Psychological and pedagogical perspectives* (pp. 115–134). Hong Kong and Melbourne: Comparative Education Research Centre, University of Hong Kong & the Australian Council for Educational Research.

Dahlgren, L. O. (1984). Outcomes of learning. In F. Marton, D. Hounsell & N. Entwistle (Eds.), *The experience of learning* (pp. 19–35). Edinburgh: Scottish Academic Press.

Donald, J. (1997). *Improving the environment for learning: Academic leaders talk about what works.* San Francisco: Jossey Bass.

Driver, R., & Erickson, G. (1983). Theories-in-action: Some theoretical and empirical issues in the study of students' conceptual frameworks. *Studies in Science Education, 10,* 37–60.

Dunkin, M. J. (Ed.). (1991). *Award-winning university teachers.* Sydney: Centre for Teaching and Learning, The University of Sydney.

Dunkin, M. J. (2002). Novice and award-winning teachers' concepts and beliefs about teaching in higher education: Effectiveness, efficacy and evaluation. In N. Hativa & P. Goodyear (Eds.), *Teacher thinking, beliefs and knowledge in higher education* (pp. 41–57). Dordrecht, the Netherlands: Kluwer Academic Publishers.

Dunkin, M. J., & Precians, R. P. (1992). Award-winning teachers' concepts of teaching. *Higher Education, 24,* 483–502.

Education and Manpower Bureau (2003). *Education statistics.* Hong Kong: Education and Manpower Bureau.

Education Commission (1999). *Learning for life.* Hong Kong Special Administrative Region: Education Commission.

Elton, L., & Partington, P. (1993). *Teaching standards and excellence in higher education. Developing a culture of quality.* Sheffield, U.K.: The U.K. Universities' Staff Development Unit.

Entwistle, N., & Ramsden, P. (1983). *Understanding student learning.* London: Croom Helm.

Feldman, K. A. (1976). The superior college teacher from the student's view. *Research in Higher Education, 5,* 243–288.

Feldman, K. A., & Newcomb, T. M. (1969). *The impact of college on students.* San Francisco: Jossey-Bass.

Feldman, K. A., & Paulsen, M. B. (Eds.). (1994). *Teaching and learning in the college classroom.* Needham Heights, MA: Ginn Press.

Freed, J. E., Klugman, M. R., & Fife, J. D. (2000). *A culture for academic excellence: Implementing the quality principles in higher education.* San Francisco: Jossey-Bass.

Galton, M., Hargreaves, L., Comber, C., Wall, D., & Pell, A. (1999). *Inside the primary classroom: 20 years on.* London: Routledge.

Galton, M., Simon, B., & Croll, P. (1980). *Inside the primary classroom.* London: Routledge & Kegan Paul.

Geertz, C. (1973). Thick description: Toward an interpretive theory of culture. In C. Geertz (Ed.), *The interpretation of cultures: Selected essays* (pp. 3–30). London: Fontana Press.

Gibbs, G., & Habeshaw, T. (2002). *Recognizing and rewarding excellent teaching.* Milton Keynes, U.K.: TQEF National Coordination Team, The Open University.

Gibbs, G., Habeshaw, S., & Habeshaw, T. (1992). *53 interesting things to do in your lectures* (4th ed.). Bristol, U.K.: Technical and Educational Services.

Glaser, B. G., & Strauss, A. L. (1967). *The discovery of grounded theory.* Chicago: Aldine.

Gow, L., & Kember, D. (1993). Conceptions of teaching and their relationship to student learning. *British Journal of Educational Psychology, 63,* 20–33.

Green, D. (1994). What is quality in higher education? Concepts, policy and practice. In D. Green (Ed.), *What is quality in higher education?* (pp. 3–20). Buckingham, U.K.: Society for Research into Higher Education & Open University Press.

Harvey, L., & Green, D. (1993). Defining quality. *Assessment and Evaluation in Higher Education, 18*(1), 9–34.

Harvey, L., & Knight, P. T. (1996). *Transforming higher education.* Buckingham, U.K.: SRHE and Open University Press.

Hattie, J., & Marsh, H.W. (1996). The relationship between research and teaching: A meta-analysis. *Review of Educational Research, 66*(4), 507–542.

Healey, M. (2000). Developing the scholarship of teaching in higher education. *Higher Education Research and Development, 19*(2), 169–189.

Helm, H., & Novak, J. D. (1983). *Misconceptions in science and mathematics.* Ithaca, NY: Cornell University Press.

Ho, D. Y. F. (1986). Chinese patterns of socialisation: A critical review. In M. H. Bond (Ed.), *The psychology of the Chinese people* (pp. 1–37). London: Oxford University Press.

Ho, D. Y. F. (1996). Filial piety and its psychological consequences. In M. H. Bond (Ed.), *The handbook of Chinese psychology* (pp. 155–166). Hong Kong: Oxford University Press.

Ho, I. T. (1999). *Teacher thinking about student problem behaviours and management strategies: A comparative study of Australian and Hong Kong teachers.* Unpublished doctoral thesis, The University of Sydney, Sydney, Australia.

Ho, I. T. (2001). Are Chinese teachers authoritarian? In D. Watkins & J. B. Biggs (Eds.), *Teaching the Chinese learner: Psychological and pedagogical perspectives* (pp. 99–114). Hong Kong and Melbourne: Comparative Education Research Centre, University of Hong Kong & the Australian Council for Educational Research.

Kaufman, D. M. & Mann, K. V. (1996). Comparing students' attitudes in problem-based and conventional curricula. *Academic Medicine, 71*(10), 1096–1099.

Kember, D. (1997). A reconceptualisation of the research into university academics' conceptions of teaching. *Learning and Instruction, 7*(3), 255–275.

Kember, D. (2001). Beliefs about knowledge and the process of teaching and learning as a factor in adjusting to study in higher education. *Studies in Higher Education, 26*(2), 205–221.

Kember, D. (2004). Interpreting student workload and the factors which shape students' perceptions of their workload. *Studies in Higher Education, 29*(2), 165–184.

Kember, D. et al (2001). *Reflective teaching and learning in the health professions.* Oxford, U.K.: Blackwell Science.

Kember, D., & Gow, L. (1994). Orientations to teaching and their effect on the quality of student learning. *Journal of Higher Education, 65*(1), 58–74.

Kember, D., & Kwan, K. P. (2000). Lecturers' approaches to teaching and their relationship to conceptions of good teaching. *Instructional Science, 28*, 469–490.

Kember, D., & Kwan, K. P. (2002). Lecturers' approaches to teaching and their relationship to conceptions of good teaching. In N. Hativa and P. Goodyear (Eds.), *Teacher thinking, beliefs and knowledge in higher education* (pp. 219–239). Dordrecht, the Netherlands: Kluwer Academic Publishers.

Kember, D., Jenkins, W., & Ng, K. C. (2003). Adult students' perceptions of good teaching as a function of their conceptions of learning – Part 1. Influencing the development of self-determination. *Studies in Continuing Education, 25*(2), 240–251.

King, P. M., & Kitchener, K. S. (1994). *Developing reflective judgement: Understanding and promoting intellectual growth and critical thinking in adolescents and adults.* San Francisco: Jossey-Bass.

Kolb, D. A. (1994). Learning styles and disciplinary differences. In K. A. Feldman & M. B. Paulsen (Eds.), *Teaching and learning in the college classroom* (pp.151–164). Needham Heights, MA: Ginn Press.

Kvale, S. (1994). Ten standard objections to qualitative research interviews. *Journal of Phenomenological Psychology, 1*(1), 1–28.

Lee, W. O. (1996). The cultural context for Chinese learners: Conceptions of learning in the Confucian tradition. In D. Watkins & J. B. Biggs (Eds.), *The Chinese learner: Cultural, psychological and contextual influences* (pp. 25–41). Melbourne and Hong Kong: Australian Council for Educational Research and the Comparative Education Research Centre, University of Hong Kong.

Lewin, K. (1952). Group decision and social change. In G. E. Swanson, T. M. Newcomb & F. E. Hartley (Eds.), *Readings in social psychology* (pp. 459–473). New York: Holt.

Lincoln, Y., & Guber, E. (1985). *Naturalistic inquiry.* Newbury Park, CA: Sage Publication.

Marsh, H. W. (1987). Students' evaluations of university teaching: Research findings, methodological issues, and directions for future research. *International Journal of Educational Research, 11,* 253–388.

Marsh, H. W., & Hattie, J. (2002). The relation between research productivity and teaching effectiveness: Complementary, antagonistic or independent constructs. *Journal of Higher Education, 73*(5), 603–641.

McDermott, L. C. (1984). Research on conceptual understanding in mechanics. *Physics Today, 37,* 24–32.

McNaught, C., & Anwyl, J. (1992). Awards for teaching excellence at Australian universities. *Higher Education Review, 25*(1), 31–44.

Morris, P. (1998). *The Hong Kong school curriculum: Development, issues and policies.* Hong Kong: Hong Kong University Press.

Morris, P., Chan, K. K., & Lo, M.L. (1998). Changing primary schools in Hong Kong: Perspectives on policy and its impact. In P. Simpson & P. Morris (Eds.), *Curriculum and assessment for Hong Kong: Two components, one system* (pp. 201–222). Hong Kong: Open University of Hong Kong Press.

Moses, I. (1990). Teaching, research and scholarship in different disciplines. *Higher Education, 19,* 351–375.

Neufeld, V. R., & Barrows, H. S. (1974). The McMaster philosophy: An approach to medical education. *Journal of Medical Education, 49*(1), 1040–1050.

Neumann, L., & Neumann, Y. (1985). Determinants of students' instructional evaluation: A comparison of four levels of academic areas. *Journal of Educational Research, 78,* 152–158.

Newble, D., & Clarke, R. (1987). Approaches to learning in a traditional and an innovative medical school. In J. T .E. Richardson, M. W. Eysenk & D. W. Piper (Eds.), *Student learning: Research in education and cognitive psychology* (pp. 39–46). Milton Keynes, U.K.: SRHE and Open University.

Nussbaum, J., & Novick, S. (1982). Alternative frameworks, conceptual conflict and accommodation: Toward a principled teaching strategy. *Instructional Science, 11,* 183–200.

NVivo qualitative data analysis program (Version 1.3) [Computer software]. (2000). Melbourne, Australia: QSR International.

Osborne, R. J., & Wittrock, M. C. (1983). Learning science: A generative process. *Science Education, 67*(4), 489–508.

Pfundt, H., & Duit, R. (1985). *Bibliography: Students' alternative frameworks and science education.* Kiel, West Germany: Institut fur die Padogogik der Naturwissenschaften.

Potter, J., & Wetherell, M. (1994). Analyzing discourse. In A. Bryman & R. G. Burgess (Eds.), *Analyzing qualitative data* (pp. 47–66). London: Routledge.

Pratt, D. D. (1992). Conceptions of teaching. *Adult Education Quarterly, 42*(4), 203–220.

Pratt, D. D., Kelly, M., & Wong, W. S. S. (1999). Chinese conceptions of "effective teaching" in Hong Kong: Towards culturally sensitive evaluations of teaching. *International Journal of Lifelong Education, 18*(4), 241–258.

Ramsden, P. (1992). *Learning to teach in higher education.* London: Routledge.

Ramsden, P., Margetson, D., Martin, E., & Clarke, S. (1995). *Recognizing and rewarding good teaching in Australian higher education.* Canberra: Australian Government Publishing Service.

Richards, T. J., & Richards, L. (1991). The NUD*IST qualitative data analysis system. *Qualitative Sociology, 14*(4), 307–324.

Salili, F. (1996). Accepting personal responsibility for learning. In D. Watkins & J. B. Biggs (Eds.), *The Chinese learner: Cultural, psychological and contextual influences* (pp. 85–105). Melbourne and Hong Kong: Australian Council for Educational Research and the Comparative Education Research Centre, University of Hong Kong.

Sheppard, C., & Gilbert, J. (1991). Course design, teaching method and student epistemology. *Higher Education, 22*, 229–249.

Shipman, M. (1981). *The limitations of social research* (2nd ed.). New York: Longman.

Stigler, J., & Hiebert, J. (1999). *The teaching gap.* New York: Free Press.

Stokes, S. F. (2001). Problem-based learning in a Chinese context: Faculty perceptions. In D. Watkins & J. B. Biggs (Eds.), *Teaching the Chinese learner: Psychological and pedagogical perspectives* (pp. 205–218). Hong Kong and Melbourne: Comparative Education Research Centre, University of Hong Kong and the Australian Council for Educational Research.

Strauss, A., & Corbin, J. (1990). *Basics of qualitative research: Grounded theory procedures and techniques.* Newbury Park, CA: Sage.

Strike, K. A., & Posner, G. J. (1985). A conceptual change view of learning and understanding. In L. H. T. West & A. L. Pines (Eds.), *Cognitive structure and conceptual change* (pp. 231–240). New York: Academic Press.

Tam, T. K. (1993). The role of quantification in qualitative research in education. *Educational Research Journal, 8*, 19–27.

Trigwell, K., Prosser, M., & Taylor, P. (1994). Qualitative differences in approaches to teaching first year university science. *Higher Education, 27*, 75–84.

Trigwell, K., Prosser, M., & Waterhouse, F. (1999). Relations between teachers' approaches to teaching and students' approaches to learning. *Higher Education, 37*, 57–70.

University Grants Committee of Hong Kong. (2003). *Facts and figures 2002*. Retrieved November 20, 2005, from http://www.ugc.edu.hk/english/documents/figures/

Watkins, D., & Biggs, J. B. (Eds.). (1996). *The Chinese learner: Cultural, psychological and contextual influences*. Melbourne and Hong Kong: Australian Council for Educational Research and the Comparative Education Research Centre, University of Hong Kong.

Watkins, D., & Biggs, J. B. (Eds.). (2001). *Teaching the Chinese learner: Psychological and pedagogical perspectives*. Hong Kong: Comparative Education Research Centre, University of Hong Kong.

Wegner, E. (1998). *Communities of practice: Learning, meaning and identity*. Cambridge, U.K.: Cambridge University Press.

West, L. (1988). Implications of recent research for improving secondary school science learning. In P. Ramsden (Ed.), *Improving learning: New perspectives* (pp. 51–68). London: Kogan Page.

West, L. H. T., & Pines, A. L. (Eds.). (1985). *Cognitive structure and conceptual change*. New York: Academic Press.

Wideen, M., Mayer-Smith, J., & Moon, B. (1998). A critical analysis of the research on learning to teach: Making the case for an ecological perspective on inquiry. *Review of Educational Research, 68*(2), 130–178.

Wu, D. Y. H. (1996). Chinese childhood socialisation. In M. H. Bond (Ed.), *The handbook of Chinese psychology* (pp. 143–154). Hong Kong: Oxford University Press.

Yin, R. K. (1994). *Case study research: Design and methods*. London: Sage.